I0429313

CREATING MONEY

How the Information Age and the Computer
Have Undermined Capitalism, and Socialism Too

by

David S. Holland

Copyright © 2011 David S. Holland
All rights reserved.

ISBN: 1461002850
ISBN-13: 9781461002857

* * *

About the Author

David S. Holland has a professional background spanning law, banking policy, and technology. He was a member of a financial industry consulting firm for ten years and then was a policy and financial analyst with the Federal Deposit Insurance Corporation. He has undergraduate and law degrees from the University of Virginia, an MBA from the College of William & Mary, a Doctor of Business Administration (DBA) from The George Washington University, and a BS in Electrical Engineering from George Mason University. He retired from the United States Army Reserve with the rank of Colonel.

* * *

Also by David S. Holland

Federal Regulation of Banking 1986-87
(Co-author with Carter H. Golembe)

When Regulation Was Too Successful—
The Sixth Decade of Deposit Insurance

Vietnam, A Memoir: Saigon Cop

Vietnam, A Memoir: Airborne Trooper

Vietnam, A Memoir: Mekong Mud Soldier

One Space Or Two—Memoirs of a Guv'mint Bur'crat

* * *

Preface

This book is a tough read. The subject matters are finance and economics, which are mind-numbing in themselves. And the focus is not on personalities. Many writers will tackle a difficult topic in areas such as finance and economics by constructing a narrative around individual players. The goal is to humanize the topic, making it more interesting and understandable to the reader. This author is not that talented.

Moreover, the author does not think the story of the financial mess, called by some the Great Recession, that surfaced in 2007-08 is primarily about human culprits. Yes, there was human malfeasance. There was certainly greed, short-sightedness, and ill-conceived actions. The principal storyline, however, involves technological advances, specifically the computer, and humankind's failure to understand the ramifications for not just finance and economics but just about everything.

The financial mess and economic troubles of the last few years are consequences of the Information Age. As its name implies, the Information Age is all about information. The Age's cause and tool, the computer, has resulted in the elevation of finance from a helpmate or lubricant for economic activity to an end in itself, an industry whose input and output are little more than forms of information, a primary form being simply money.

No grand solution is proposed in this book. The focus is on the development of what seems to be an over-sized financial industry. In that sense, it is more of a history than a policy guide. But good policy begins with an understanding of history. Perhaps others will take the further step of suggesting policies for the changed world that the Information Age is producing.

The U.S. banking industry lost a friend in 2010. A World War II veteran, Dr. Carter H. Golembe was a writer, historian, and consultant. For much of the last forty years of the 20th Century, his insightful commentaries on industry issues and trends were fundamental contributions to the policy dialogues. His even-handed analyses are sorely missed. This book is dedicated to his memory.

David S. Holland
February 2011

* * *

Table of Contents

Charts

Tables

I

Welcome to the Information Age

What caused the financial difficulties that exploded on the world's economies in 2007-2008 and that in the United States produced the Great Recession? Providing mortgages to unqualified borrowers has been blamed. So have complex financial instruments and strategies that few understood, and weird financial insurance products with names like credit default swaps. Also lax supervision, unfocused regulation, greed on Wall Street, greed on Main Street, accounting rules, maybe laissez faire government, maybe over-reaching government, probably some ideological hostility to government oversight in general, and much more.

In January 2011, the Financial Crisis Inquiry Commission, the ten-member government commission created to investigate what happened, issued a six hundred-plus page report that focused on largely micro-level and cyclical factors.[1] The report was not unanimous and, as with many things Washingtonian, reflected political and ideological divisions. The six Democrats dwelt on human mistakes, misjudgments, misdeeds. Three Republican dissenting members concentrated on credit bubbles and market forces. A fourth Republican dissenting member found fault with government's subsidization activities in the housing market. An unkind review of the report characterized it as "not an investigative trilogy but a left-leaning essay collection, a right-leaning Power-Point presentation and a colorful far-right magazine."[2] Catchy, but perhaps a bit harsh. The three analyses did have areas of agreement, the significant differences seeming to be matters of emphasis and interpretation.

But none of the three views expressed in the report spent much time, if any, on the really big picture, the macroeconomic-level context. In that macro context are the rise in the importance of finance—a phenomenon that might be called the financialization of the economy—and the reason the rise has occurred.[3] For most of its time as a component of human history, finance served largely as a lubricant and a fuel for economic activity. The lubrication was provided by the payment systems that enabled accounts to be maintained, funds to be transferred between parties, and obligations to be settled. The fuel was in the form of loans and other advances of funds that enabled individuals and businesses to produce and market products and services, and consumers to purchase those products and services.

Today, however, finance is more than a lubricant and a fuel. It is now an end in itself, a product and service overshadowing all but a few others. The move from support role to center stage was not a sudden thing. Indeed, the process has been ongoing for centuries as economic activity expanded geographically beyond local markets to include national and international commerce. But a relatively recent—in historical terms—technological development has accelerated the growth of finance. As the financial difficulties that surfaced in 2007-08 have highlighted, this acceleration has not been without negative consequences. And in turn, the negative consequences have caused at least some observers to question traditional ideas on how economies operate.

The new technological development is the computer. The impact of the computer on humankind is acknowledged by such terms as the Information Age. But accepting that humankind has entered a new era and understanding what that new era entails, and threatens, do not necessarily go hand-in-hand.

Complex financial assets and strategies were made possible by the computer and certainly were in their own right a significant contributor to the chaos that surfaced in 2007-08. But the cause and effect relationship between the computer and the recent, and ongoing, financial troubles is much more complicated. Complexity has actually served to mask the primary impact of the computer. That primary impact is money creation. The computer is a money-creating machine of the first order.

How so?

Start with the name of the new era: the Information Age. The raw material of the Information Age is in the name: information—kilobytes, megabytes, gigabytes, terabytes, petabytes, exabytes, and eventually more of information. The tool that processes and manipulates the information is the computer. And the product that is produced? Still more information. Roughly, the Information Age—the time when computers became commonplace in homes and the workplace—can be dated to the early 1980s and is entering its fourth decade.[4] The sector of the economy that has grown the most during this period, that has thus in one sense "benefited" the most from the tsunami of information, is the financial sector.[5]

And why has the financial sector benefited the most? Because the financial sector is all about information, information about money and wealth, about how to acquire money and wealth, about ways to create and preserve money and wealth. At one level, money and wealth are interchangeable, synonymous. Where they are not, wealth can usually be measured in terms of money. Ultimately, money—itself or as a measure of wealth—is nothing more than information: information about supply and demand, information about wants and desires. So a tool—the computer—that produces an endless supply of information is married to an industry—finance—that is information intensive if not solely about information and, more importantly, that actually creates a particular type of information, that type being money. The result is a money-creating phenomenon for which the world's economic system, geared toward money as a scarce commodity, was not and is not prepared.

This book is an examination of the symbiotic relationship between the computer and finance. The topics considered include the growth of finance as a result of the relationship, how the relationship has operated, and the impacts on and for the economic system.

A New Type of Engineer

If someone had been asked thirty years ago about the profession of financial engineering, he or she would have likely responded with an uncomprehending "Huh?" Data on the growth of the financial sector over the last several decades is presented in numbing detail in the next chapter. For the moment, however, the game-changing nature of what has occurred might be grasped by focusing on the rise of a whole new engineering discipline linking the computer and finance. Indeed, perhaps nothing better epitomizes the fundamental change that has taken place in the financial world over the last three decades than the rise of this new profession of financial engineering.

What is financial engineering? One simple Internet-supplied definition is, "[t]he creation of new and improved financial products through innovative design or repackaging of existing financial instruments," which sounds innocuous enough.[6] In 2009 the Department of Finance at the University of Illinois was offering on its website a somewhat more formidable definition, actually two of them.[7] First, "Financial engineering is the application of the mathematical tools commonly used in physics and engineering to financial problems, especially the pricing and hedging of derivative instruments." The second definition was "the use of financial instruments such as forwards, futures, swaps, options, and related products to restructure or rearrange cash flows in order to achieve particular financial goals, particularly the management of financial risk." Another term for such financial instruments, a term that has often surfaced in analyses of the Great Recession and that will appear often in the pages ahead, is derivatives.

"Mathematical tools commonly used in physics and engineering...." By the latter portion of the 20th Century, the application of mathematical tools used in physics and engineering entailed—no, more than entailed, required—the use of computers. Similarly, the use of these mathematical tools in finance only became feasible on a large scale when the computational power of computers became generally accessible. The cause and effect equation can be simplified: computers begat financial engineering.

The University of Illinois' Department of Finance had little doubt, at least in 2009, about the birthplace of financial engineering.[8] It was Chicago. On May 16th, 1972, the Chicago Mercantile Exchange offered the "first financial futures products, currency futures." On April 26, 1973, the Chicago Board Options Exchange began offering the "first exchange-traded options." In the words of the Illini Department of Finance, "These two events revolutionized financial management."

But common usage of the term "financial engineering" did not coincide with the appearance of financial futures and options on the Chicago exchanges. Writing in 1988, David Warsh, then with *The Boston Globe* and now the proprietor of the website EconomicPrincipals.com, stated that the phrase "financial engineering" had become common only in the preceding ten years, and then mostly overseas. He went on to observe that a computer search revealed "a wide variety of meanings of the term in current usage, ranging from slick practices to marketing palaver to dignified intellectual enterprises."[9] One of Google's cute little tools confirms Warsh's conclusion about the rise of the phrase. Plugging "financial engineering," with the quotation marks, into the Google News archive search tool produces about 19 hits for the period 1960-69, 17 for 1970-1979, 74 for 1980-1989, and 266 for 1990-1999.[10]

Nicholas F. Brady, Treasury Secretary for a few months under Ronald Reagan and then for the full term of George H.W. Bush, appears to have been one of the earliest officials in the United States Government to speak of financial engineering. In testimony before Congress in February 1989 cautioning against measures to curb debt-financed corporate takeovers, Mr. Brady said that he was concerned about the amount of talent going into "financial engineering" rather than into production and job creation. Nevertheless, he saw no proof that the economy had sustained damage.[11]

In his 1988 *Boston Globe* article, Warsh drew an analogy between civil and mechanical engineering on one hand and financial engineering on the other.[12] The field of financial engineering could be viewed as in a similar position to civil and mechanical engineering in the 19th Century. Then, skyscrapers, elevators, and engines of various types were in their infancy. Enormous projects were completed: the Niagara Falls hydraulic station, complex waterworks systems for major cities, the Brooklyn Bridge, Cyrus Field's trans-Atlantic cable, railroads galore. There were failures, both financial and physical, and there was government involvement, notably to investigate the failures and see to their correction. But the failures were but brief pauses on a journey of improvement for the human animal.

Warsh was writing in the aftermath of the market crash on October 19 and 20 of the preceding year, 1987, a crash due to computerized trading strategies. The official report of the Presidential body set up to examine the crisis, the Brady Commission Task Force, had just been released.[13] Warsh saw the report as simply calling for better engineering of the system for trading financial instruments. Outright prohibitions of such things as dynamic hedging and index arbitrage were not suggested. Instead, the report focused on the need for a unified clearing system and means to slow trading and dampen volatility when markets became overheated. And this Warsh, and presumably others, seemed to consider proper. As were civil and mechanical engineering 150 years before, financial engineering in 1988 was likely "on the verge of a dramatic takeoff into mastery of its world."[14] Government's role, as the Brady Commission envisioned, was not to prohibit things but to provide guidance and structure.

And as for the computer, the instrument that had produced the market crash of October 1987, Warsh was optimistic: "In all likelihood, the computer poses no more fundamental threat to safety in markets than the railroad engine did to safety in transport."[15] He envisioned financial engineering going through a slow and sometimes painful learning process, and he acknowledged that the failure of a financial entity could have much wider impacts than the failure of, say, a bridge. But overall he saw financial engineering following a path of growth, success, and social betterment similar to the path that had been followed by civil and mechanical engineering.

So, is the computer the controllable tool of financial engineering that Warsh, and many others since, envisioned? That is the question that underlies this book and that resurfaces in various guises in the pages ahead.

Education

To achieve respectability, a new profession must be represented in academia. Ideally, it should become a full-fledged academic discipline, whatever that nebulous designation may mean. Finance had been a part of academia, including business school curriculums, well prior to the 1990s. Three pillars of modern finance, each heavily mathematical, are modern portfolio theory (MPT), the capital asset pricing model (CAPM), and option pricing models.

Harry Markowitz introduced modern portfolio theory in the 1950s, his initial major work appearing in 1952.[16] In modern portfolio theory, the goal is to maximum the return on investments while minimizing risk. The tool to achieve the goal is diversification. The means, well, that's the role of the heavy mathematics.

From the work of Markowitz and others in modern portfolio theory flowed the capital asset pricing model. Attributed to the independent efforts of William Sharpe, Jack Treynor, John Lintner, and Jan Mossin, the CAPM appeared in the early to mid-1960s. At its simplest, the model prices a single security in a portfolio. The simplest, however, quickly gives way to such matters as security market lines, systematic risk (beta), efficient frontiers, risk-free rates of return, and of course, heavy mathematics.

But just ahead was some really, really heavy mathematics. In 1973, Fischer Black, Myron Scholes, and Robert Merton produced an option pricing model. Black and Scholes published the initial paper.[17] Merton expanded upon their work and also provided the nomenclature: Black-Scholes option pricing model.[18] The model opened the door to partial differential equations, geometric Brownian motions, standard normal cumulative distribution functions, probability density functions, multiple Greek identifiers, Monte Carlo simulations, stochastic volatility, and much else well beyond high school algebra, geometry, and even trigonometry.

Thus in the several decades preceding the 1990s, college and university finance and business programs had much to impart. But the body of financial knowledge required on Wall Street—not necessarily in the top positions but certainly at the operational level—was expanding rapidly. Derivatives—financial assets that derive their value from other financial assets—were becoming more prominent. Financial engineering was achieving recognition if not as a full-fledged profession at least as a field of substantial endeavor. A greater role for academia was perceived.

7

And academia responded. An estimate on the website of Baruch College of the City University of New York is that approximately 60 universities in the United States added Masters in Financial Engineering programs between 1994 and 2008.[19] The number might overstate the new programs that actually use the term "Financial Engineering."[20] Master of Finance also appears to be a common nomenclature for a degree in the field. In addition, a number of schools have expanded undergraduate offerings in areas with names like computational finance. The new graduate and undergraduate programs are found in business schools of universities, in finance departments, and even in mathematics departments. Several oft-mentioned institutions that have expanded efforts in financial engineering, though not necessarily using the term "financial engineering," are the aforementioned Baruch College, the Sloan School of Business at New York University, Carnegie Mellon University, Harvard Business School, and Massachusetts Institute of Technology's Sloan School of Management. A complete list of institutions that have recognized in some way the increasing quantification of finance would likely include just about everybody.

Postmortem

The Information Age is certainly not over, and financial engineering, while perhaps discredited a bit, is certainly an entrenched component of the financial system. So attempting a final postmortem on either would be very much premature. But an interim postmortem, something in the nature of a mid-term evaluation following the largest economic downturn of the Information Age, would not seem inappropriate. And some really impressive names have offered some very negative comments.

Warren Buffett, investor extraordinaire, was in with an early evaluation, indeed somewhat of a prognostication. In the 2002 *Annual Report* of Berkshire Hathaway Inc., he described derivatives as "financial weapons of mass destruction, carrying dangers that, while now latent, are potentially lethal."[21]

Paul Samuelson won the 1970 Nobel Prize in economics and was author of *Economics*, for decades the most commonly used undergraduate economics textbook. Shortly before his death in December 2009, he had this to say on the end-of-decade recession: "I thought from the beginning this was going to be very serious because it was people like me—people at MIT and Chicago—who created all these wonderful derivatives. The way they were formulated by financial engineers, they were not understood by any CEO. They didn't even know who they were in the bathtub with."[22]

Robert Merton was one of the originators of the Black-Scholes option pricing model, for which he shared the 1997 Nobel Prize in Economics. As noted earlier, the Black-Scholes model is one of the foundations of financial engineering. In 1998, Mr. Merton was on the board of directors of Long-Term Capital Management, a hedge fund that used complex financial models in its operations and that failed in that year with system-rattling impact. As early as 1994, he had cautioned that "any virtue can become a vice if taken to extreme, and just so with the application of mathematical models in finance practice." [23] In a lecture at MIT in March of 2009 and in a later interview, he discussed the end-of-decade crisis. One of his conclusions: "We've created instruments for manipulating financial risk without a thorough understanding of the underlying engineering." [24]

Paul Volcker was Chairman of the Federal Reserve Board from 1979 to 1987. Since leaving the Fed he has held prominent positions in both the public and private sectors and in 2009 was appointed by President Barack Obama as head of the President's Economic Recovery Advisory Board.

In an interview in late 2009, Mr. Volcker told a tale of being at a conference a few years earlier and listening to a speaker extol the virtues of financial engineering. He found himself sitting next to a Nobel Prize winner. Mr. Volcker nudged the gentleman and asked him what financial engineering actually did for the economy and for productivity.

> Much to my surprise, he leaned over and whispered in my ear that it does nothing—and this was from a leader in the world of financial engineering. I asked him what it did do, and he said that it moves around the rents in the financial system—and besides, it's a lot of intellectual fun.

Now, I have no doubts that it moves around the rents in the financial system, but not only this, as it seems to have vastly increased them.[25]

Lastly, Alan Greenspan. Poor Alan. Chairman of the Federal Reserve Board from 1987 to 2006, Mr. Greenspan had a decidedly libertarian bent. As a regulator of the financial system for almost two decades, he was very hands-offish, believing that the system largely regulated itself. In the late 1990s he successfully led efforts against an attempt by Commodity Futures Trading Commission Chairman Brooksley Born to investigate fast-growing over-the-counter markets in newer types of derivatives. By the time he left the Fed in 2006, Mr. Greenspan had achieved a stature of almost mythical proportions. Many viewed him as the preeminent central banker in the history of the Federal Reserve.

The events of the subsequent few years significantly tarnished that reputation. On October 23, 2008, Mr. Greenspan testified before a Congressional Committee, the House Committee on Oversight and Government Reform. He was raked over the coals by legislators who had fawned over him less than two years earlier. And he responded with much, though not quite total, contrition. He conceded "flaw" in his market ideology. He acknowledged that the market for credit default swaps, a particular virulent type of derivative, needed restraint. He said: "Those of us who have looked to the self-interest of lending institutions to protect shareholders' equity, myself included, are in a state of shocked disbelief." And, "This crisis has turned out to be much broader than anything I could have imagined. It has morphed from one gripped by liquidity restraints to one in which fears of insolvency are now paramount."[26]

But such statements of contrition and acknowledgements that the brave new world created by the marriage of computers and finance is less than a benign place do not mean that the genie is back in the bottle. A consensus on why finance went astray and how it should be corralled has yet to develop. Perhaps part of the problem is that the role of the computer has been only obliquely recognized.

Boom and Bust Passé?

But wait, the reader might counter. What of the boom and bust interpretation of financial history? Can't recent events be viewed as just another boom and bust, meaning now that the bust has wiped out the excesses of the 21st Century's first boom, humans can start working toward the next boom?

Certainly the boom and bust cycle has been central in the economic history of the last few centuries. But cycles are not identical. For one thing—a most important thing—technology, a key component of economic activity, is not static. Economists who think they have a good handle on the boom-bust cycle, on the causes, the warning signs, the necessary corrective actions, are often like those military planners who are preparing for the last war. Changes wrought by technology—changes not just in military weaponry and equipment but also in how society operates, in how people communicate, in how cultures evolve—can make the next war very different from the last. Similarly, technological change can render the next boom-bust cycle far different than its predecessor.

To put it another way, yes, booms and busts over the decades and centuries have had many commonalities. But technological change has often been one of those commonalities. Get the contradiction, or maybe paradox? Change is a constant. And technological change can hinder, except in hindsight, recognition of those commonalities of human nature that do not change, such as greed and irrational exuberance. Which helps explain what the computer has wrought, in spades.

The remaining chapters in this book investigate the impact of—some might say havoc wrought by—the computer in the field of finance. Chapter 2 presents the numbers, that is, data on the financialization of the economy. Chapter 3 highlights the computer's role in financialization and describes some of the players and instruments that are at the center of the activity. Chapter 4 tackles the impact of financialization—and consequently the computer—on a key element of the financial system: fractional reserve banking. Chapter 5 finds evidence of the computer's impact on finance, and of humans' difficulty in grasping the changes being wrought by the Information Age, in what may appear to be an unlikely place: the patent system. Chapter 6 attempts to grasp the Big Picture, the Meanings, the Economic Forest that is obscured by the concentration on the financial trees. And Chapter 7 looks at financial supervision and oversight for the 21st Century.

* * *

2

Financialization

The basic fact is that for several decades—decades that coincided with the computerization of society, with the rise of the Information Age— the financial sector has been the fastest growing sector of the economy. In this chapter, that growth is numbingly detailed. The examination is divided into four sections. The first tackles some definitional matters. The second looks at debt and financial assets through the prism of the U.S. Federal Reserve Board's Flow of Funds data. In the third, the exponential growth of financial derivatives, which may be thought of as contingency or insurance products, is highlighted. And the fourth focuses on the profits of the financial industry as compared to nonfinancial, and largely tangible, industries.

Debt and Financial Assets—Definitions

Economists and financial analysts are not the only individuals to know what debt is. In a modern economy, most individuals and institutions are personally acquainted with debt. For individuals, the relationship might be in the form of a mortgage on a home, or through the use of a credit card. Very few people go through life without at some point owing money to someone, or more likely to some institution. The money owed is debt. An individual or institution that owes money is referred to by terms such as debtor, borrower, or issuer. The latter term, issuer, attaches to an institution that borrows by selling financial instruments—bonds, for example. The outstanding debt of an individual or an institution is the total of the money that the individual or institution owes.

Leverage is a term that is often associated with, and is sometimes a synonym for, debt. More correctly, leverage refers to the use of debt to increase returns on investment. The possibility of increased returns comes with an increase in risk: returns might be greater, but any losses might also be greater.

Compared to the term debt, the term financial assets is somewhat fuzzier, and becoming more so as financial engineers continue pushing the envelope on new concepts and products. Plain vanilla financial assets for an individual or institution include checking and savings deposits in banks and any stocks—more formally, corporate equities—and bonds owned. Among the financial assets in the Federal Reserve's Flow of Funds data are checkable deposits and currency, time and savings deposits, money market shares, corporate and agency bonds, corporate equities, and mutual fund shares. The situation can be confusing, especially for those without an exposure to accounting. For example, an individual's deposit in a bank is a financial asset of the individual but a financial liability of the bank. Similarly, a mortgage granted by a bank to an individual is a financial asset of the bank but a financial liability of the individual.

Fuzziness regarding the term financial assets—a fuzziness that can also extend to the term debt—arises in part from a variety of financial products that are not quite full-fledged financial assets but have the potential to produce financial assets, or maybe just assets, for one of the contracting parties. For the other contracting party, a product often has the potential for producing debt, at least of the momentary variety until the contract is fulfilled. These financial products are broadly termed derivatives and mostly fall into the categories of futures, options, and swaps. Many of the products serve an insurance or hedging function, guarding against contingencies such as adverse change in the value of a full-fledged financial asset. A particular type of derivative, the credit default swap, played a prominent role to the growth of the financial sector in the first decade of the 21st Century, and in the collapse that followed. Data on not-quite financial assets are presented latter in this chapter.

The reader's understanding of the terms debt and financial assets having been sufficiently muddied, he or she should now be ready for some real numbers.

Debt and Financial Assets—Data

The Flow of Funds accounts are published quarterly by the Federal Reserve Board. The accounts record the acquisition of tangible and financial assets, and the incurrence of liabilities, throughout the U.S. economy. The accounts document the sources of funds used to acquire those assets and measure the value of assets and liabilities at the end of each quarter. The data from which the accounts are constructed come from a variety of public and private sources. The Flow of Funds accounts are one of three sets of accounts providing broad statistical descriptions of the U.S. economy, the other two being the national income and product accounts and the balance of payments accounts, both produced by the Department of Commerce.[1]

Three trends in the Flow of Funds data, as augmented by the accounts maintained by the Department of Commerce, portray a U.S. economy that is increasingly financial. First, since the early 1980s, roughly the start of the Information Age, financial assets and debt in the U.S. economy have increased at a faster rate than has gross domestic product (GDP). Second, for over 60 years, since 1945, the proportions of the nation's financial assets and debt held by the financial sector itself have grown. And third, within the financial sector the proportion of financial assets held by traditional financial intermediaries has declined as the proportion held by a variety of new institutions has increased. These trends are detailed in Charts 1 through 5.

From 1945 to the early 1980s, the relationship between total financial assets in the United States and the nation's GDP was stable (Chart 1). For those years, financial assets ranged between 4 and 5 times GDP. Beginning in the early 1980s, the relationship changed. As a multiple of GDP, financial assets began to increase, reaching over 10 times GDP in 2007. Similarly, between 1945 and the early 1980s, total debt in the United States was fairly stable at approximately 1.5 times GDP (Chart 1). Over the next twenty-five years the multiple more than doubled. In 2007, total U.S. debt was 3.5 times GDP. Stated another way, since the early 1980s, the increases in both financial assets and debt have outpaced the growth in GDP.

Chart 1: Financial Assets and Debt as Multiples of U.S. GDP

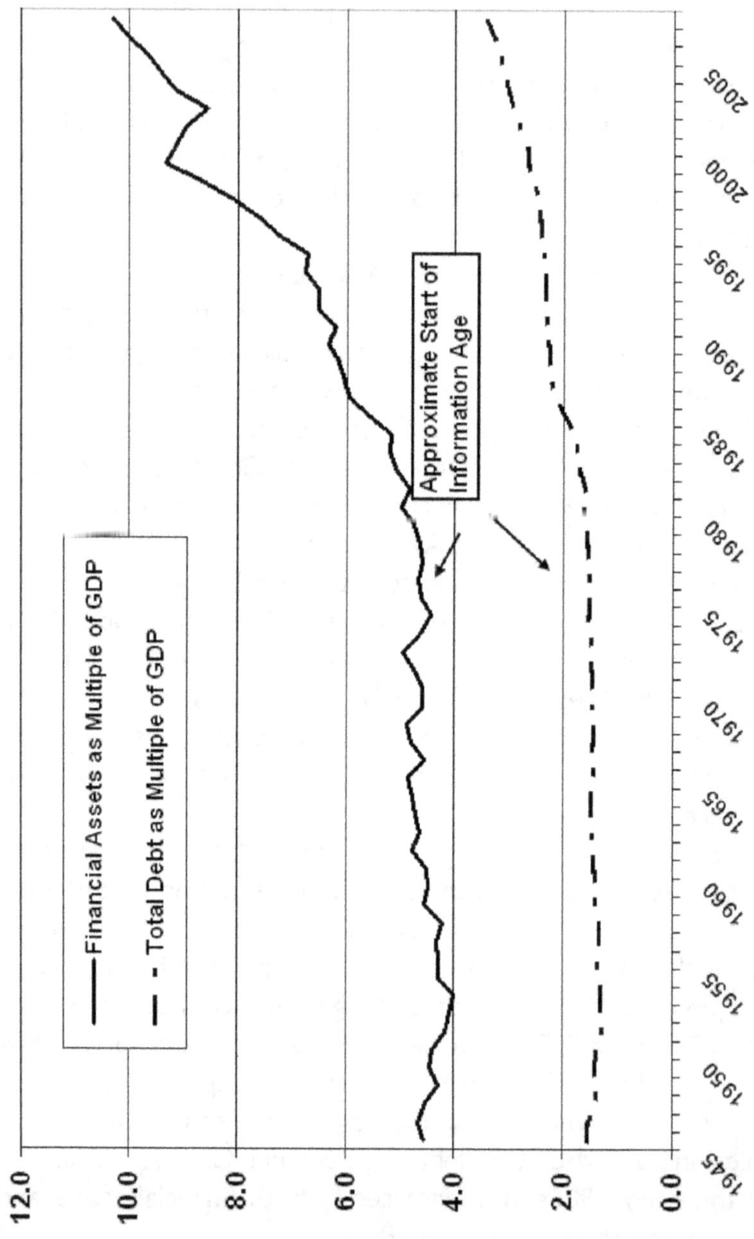

Financial Assets as Multiple of GDP

Total Debt as Multiple of GDP

Approximate Start of Information Age

Source: Federal Reserve System, "Flow of Funds Accounts of the United States."

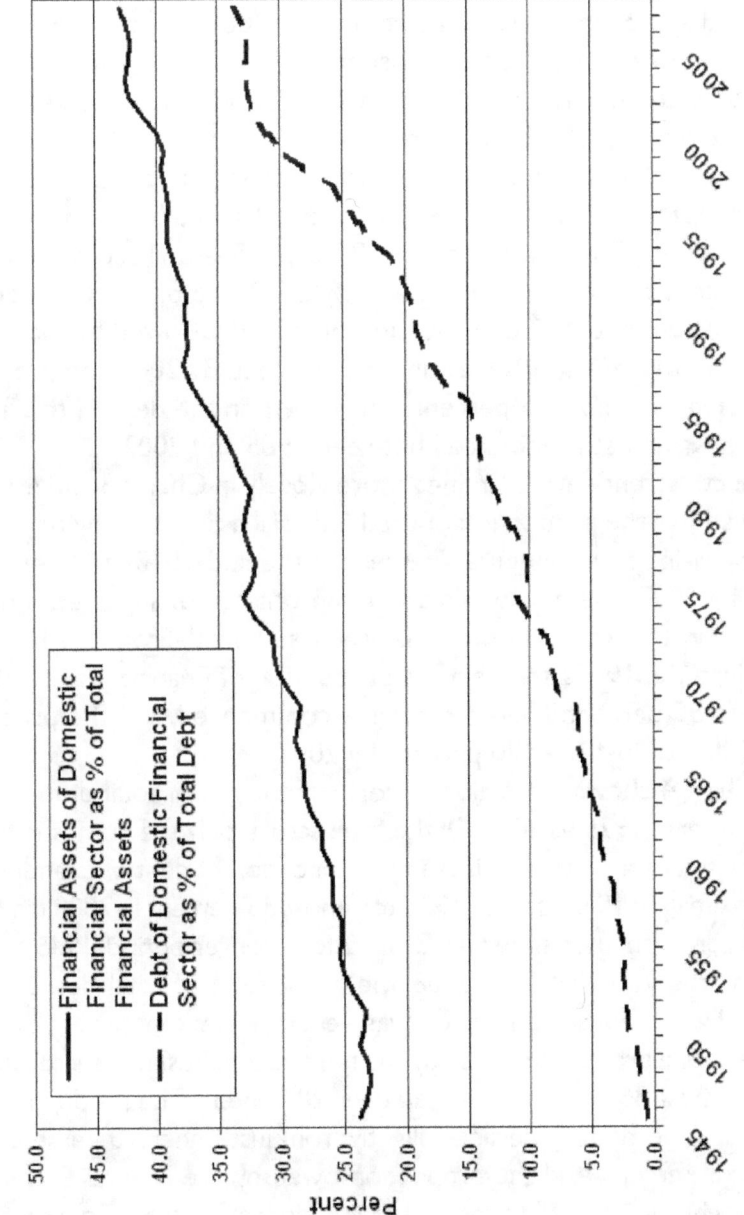

Chart 2: Growth of the Financial Sector of the U.S. Economy

Legend:
Financial Assets of Domestic Financial Sector as % of Total Financial Assets
Debt of Domestic Financial Sector as % of Total Debt

Source: Federal Reserve System, "Flow of Funds Accounts of the United States."

17

Very broadly, holders of financial assets and obligors of debt can be divided into the financial and nonfinancial sectors of the economy. The financial sector includes banks, thrift institutions, credit unions, mutual funds, money market funds, pension funds, and a growing number of variations thereof. The nonfinancial sector includes households, nonprofit organizations, nonfinancial businesses, and government, both federal and local. In the United States, the financial sector has held a steadily growing proportion of financial assets and owed a steadily growing proportion of debt (Chart 2). In the late 1940s, the financial sector held under 25 percent of total financial assets. By 2007, the proportion had risen to over 40 percent. The proportion of total debt owed by the financial sector in the late 1940s was under 3 percent. By 2007, the proportion had risen to almost 35 percent. The growth in the debt of the financial sector was most pronounced between 1985 and 2002.

Sector trends are examined more closely in Charts 3 and 4. Chart 3 again shows the proportion of total financial assets held by the financial sector rising from under 25 percent in the late 1940s to over 40 percent by 2007. The household and nonprofit sector incurred the major decline in the proportion of financial assets held. From the late 1940s well into the 1960s, this sector's proportion of financial assets hovered around 55 percent. Then the decline commenced, and the proportion had fallen to just over 30 percent by 2007.

Chart 4 shows the major sector percentages of total domestic debt for the years 1975 to 2008. Of the five sectors, only the domestic financial sector shows a sustained rise in the proportion of debt outstanding, from approximately 10 percent in 1975 to almost 35 percent in 2008 (this rise is a portion of the rise shown in Chart 2 for a longer period, 1945 to 2007). During the years 1975 to 2008, the proportion of total domestic debt owed by the household sector was generally static between 25 and 30 percent. The proportion owed by the nonfinancial business sector declined from almost 35 percent to a little over 20 percent. The proportion owed by local governments declined slightly from just under 10 percent to just under 5 percent. And the proportion owed by the Federal Government rose slightly from 1975 to the mid-1990s (approximately 17 percent to just over 20 percent), declined significantly from 1995 (20 percent) to 2001 (12 percent), and remained at approximately that level through 2008.

Chart 3: Sector Percentages of U.S. Financial Assets

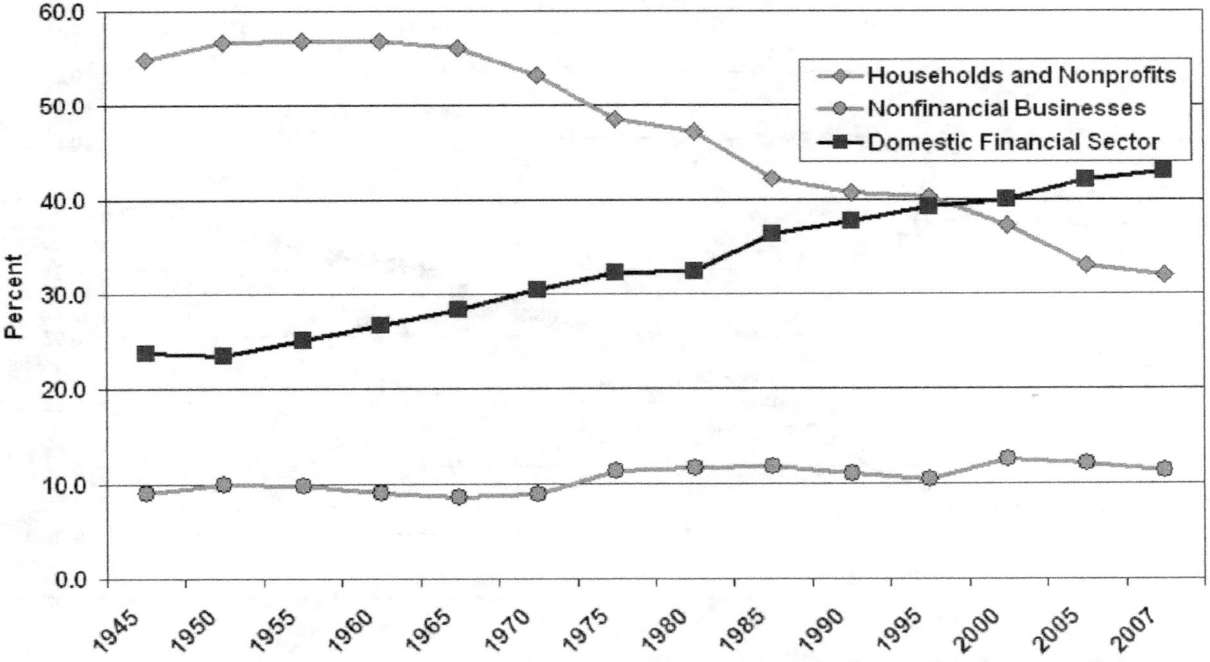

Households and Nonprofits
Nonfinancial Businesses
Domestic Financial Sector

Percent

1945 1950 1955 1960 1965 1970 1975 1980 1985 1990 1995 2000 2005 2007

60.0 50.0 40.0 30.0 20.0 10.0 0.0

Note: Government and foreign sectors omitted (the combined percentage of local and federal government sectors fell from 5.7 percent in 1945 to 2.2 percent in 2007; the percent of financial assets held by foreign holders increased from 1.6 percent in 1945 to 10.9 percent in 2007).

Source: U.S. Census Bureau, Statistical Abstract of the United States, 2009, Table 1129.

Chart 4: Sector Percentages of U.S. Domestic Debt

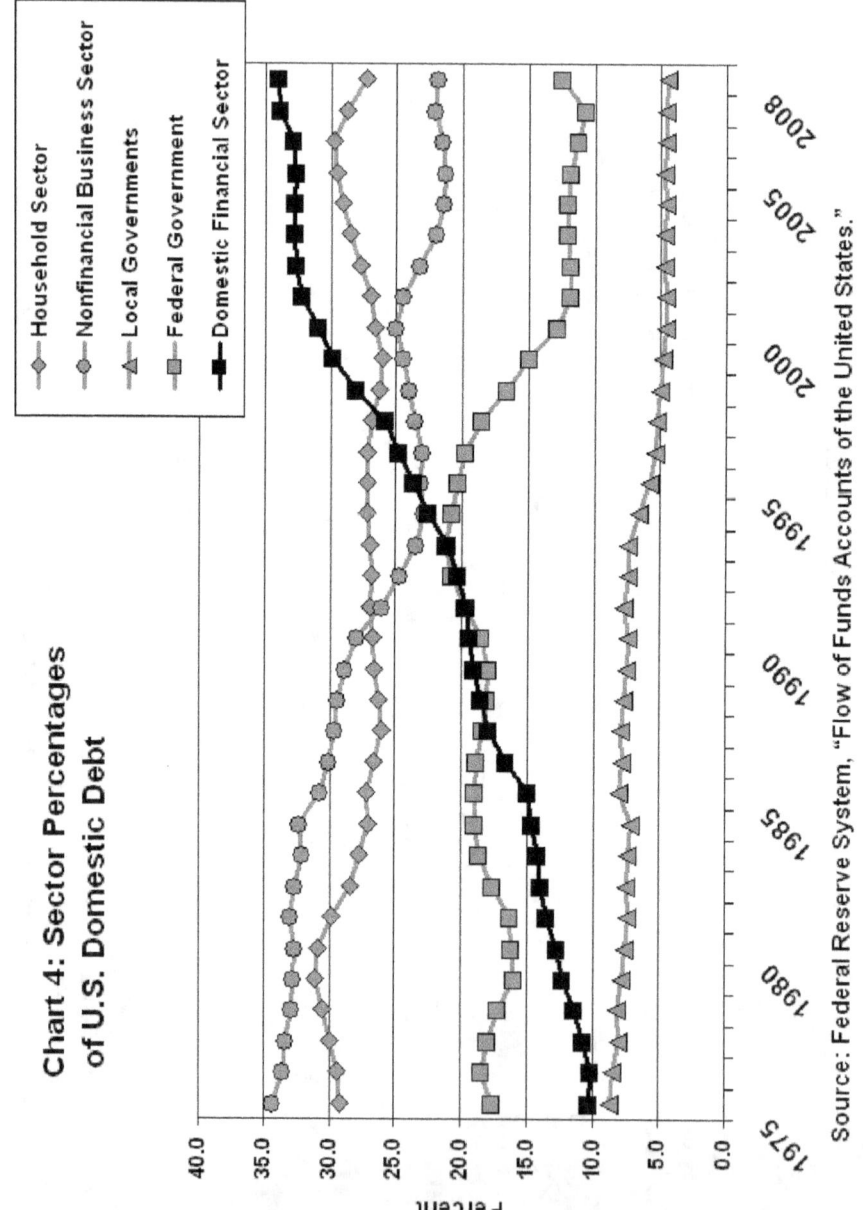

Source: Federal Reserve System, "Flow of Funds Accounts of the United States."

Much commentary on the current economic problems has focused on the increases in the debt of the household and Federal Government sectors of the economy. But the domestic financial sector's increase in the proportion of total domestic debt outstanding shows that the domestic financial sector has been the true engine of debt growth. The story told by the proportionate increases is confirmed by the absolute increases. Between 1975 and 2008, the outstanding debt of the household sector increased by a factor of 19 (from $734 billion to $13,821 billion). The outstanding debt of the Federal Government increased by a factor of 10 (from $219 billion to $2,240 billion). And leading the pack, the outstanding debt of the domestic financial sector increased by a factor of 66 (from $260 billion to $17,217 billion).

Chart 5, the final chart in the series, drills into the financial sector a bit. What the chart shows is that within the financial sector, traditional financial institutions have given ground proportionally to a growing variety of alternatives. In 1945, the proportion of the financial sector's financial assets held by traditional financial intermediaries—banks, savings institutions, credit unions, and insurance companies—was over 90 percent. By 2007, the proportion had declined to 43 percent. In 2007, the non-traditional component of the financial sector, the "New Guys," held more than half of the financial sector's financial assets. Among the New Guys are mutual funds, money market funds, government-sponsored enterprises (GSEs), agency- and GSE-backed mortgage pools, asset-backed securities issuers, and finance companies.

The New Guys include some, perhaps most, of the components of what has come to be called the shadow banking system.[2] The shadow banking system refers to financial intermediaries that perform maturity, credit, and liquidity transformations but do not have access to central bank liquidity or public sector credit guarantees.

Several aspects of Chart 5 are worth noting. From 1945 to the early 1980s, the relative decline of traditional financial intermediaries and rise of the New Guys were gradual. Then, as the Information Age kicked in, the decline of the traditional and the rise of the new accelerated. By 2000, the cross-over had occurred: the New Guys held a greater proportion of the financial sector's financial assets than did traditional financial intermediaries.

Chart 5: The Changing U.S. Financial Sector
(Percent of Total Financial Assets of the Financial Sector)

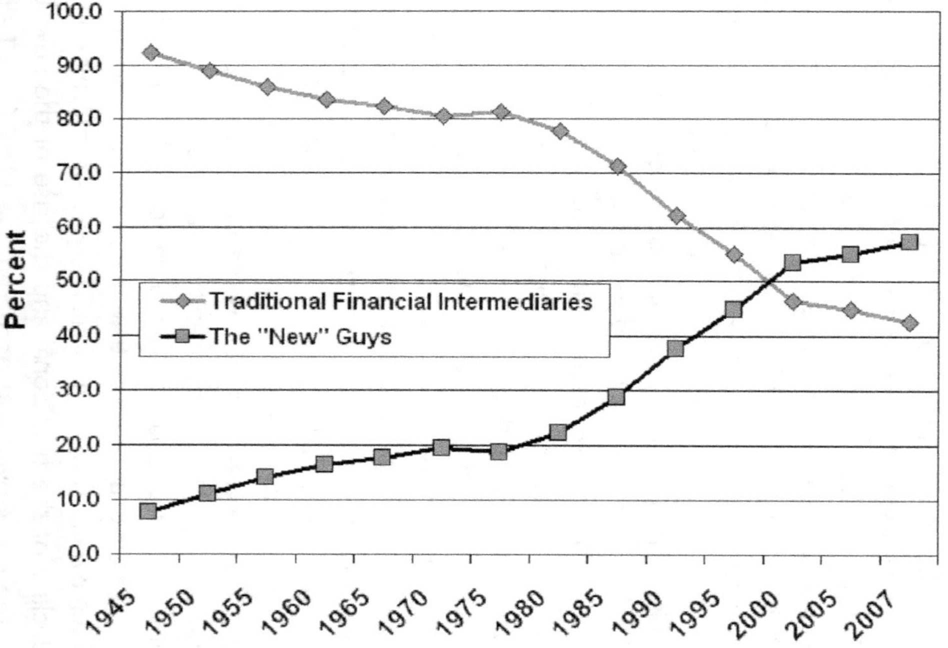

Traditional Financial Intermediaries: Banks, Savings Institutions, Credit Unions, Insurance Companies

The "New" Guys: Private Pension Funds, Government Retirement Funds, Money Market Mutual Funds, Mutual Funds, Closed-End Funds, Exchange-Traded Funds, Government-Sponsored Enterprises, Agency- and GSE-Backed Mortgage Pools, Asset-Backed Securities Issuers, Finance Companies, Real Estate Investment Trusts, Securities Brokers and Dealers, Funding Corporations

Source: U.S. Census Bureau, Statistical Abstract of the United States, 2009, Table 1129.

To repeat the assertion about trends regarding financial assets and debt in the United States, the story told by Charts 1 through 5 is three-fold. First, since the early 1980s, roughly the start of the Information Age, financial assets and debt outstanding in the U.S. economy have increased at a faster rate than has gross domestic product (Chart 1). Second, for over 60 years, since 1945, the proportions of the nation's financial assets and debt held by the financial sector itself have grown (Charts 2-4). Third, within the financial sector the proportion of financial assets held by traditional financial intermediaries has declined as the proportion held by a variety of new institutions has increased (Chart 5).

In short, the nation's debts and financial assets have risen faster than economic activity in general. The financial sector's proportions of those debts and financial assets have increased, meaning that financial sector has been the greatest user and beneficiary of its own products. The most significant growth in debts and financial assets has occurred since the early 1980s, the time generally viewed as when the computer-based Information Age really kicked in. Meanwhile, the other sectors' proportions of the nation's debts and financial assets have remained static or fallen.

The Explosive Growth of Derivatives

Total debt and total financial assets have been growing faster than the "real" or "tangible" portion of the economy for at least several decades, but the rates of debt and financial asset growth have not been outrageous—on an annual basis, maybe only a few percentage points faster. For other financial products and instruments that are not easily classified as debt or financial assets, however, growth has been explosive. These not-quite financial assets, many with insurance or insurance components and most built upon standard financial assets, are also known as derivatives, and for the most part are not in the Federal Reserve's Flow of Fund data.

Data on derivatives are among the data compiled by the Bank for International Settlements in Basel, Switzerland. The BIS is an international organization that fosters international monetary and financial cooperation and serves as a bank for central banks. Chart 6 portrays the growth of derivative financial instruments traded on organized exchanges—futures and options—from 1986 and to 2009. BIS data for over-the-counter derivatives does not go back that far. Chart 7 portrays the growth of over-the-counter derivatives from 1998 to 2009.

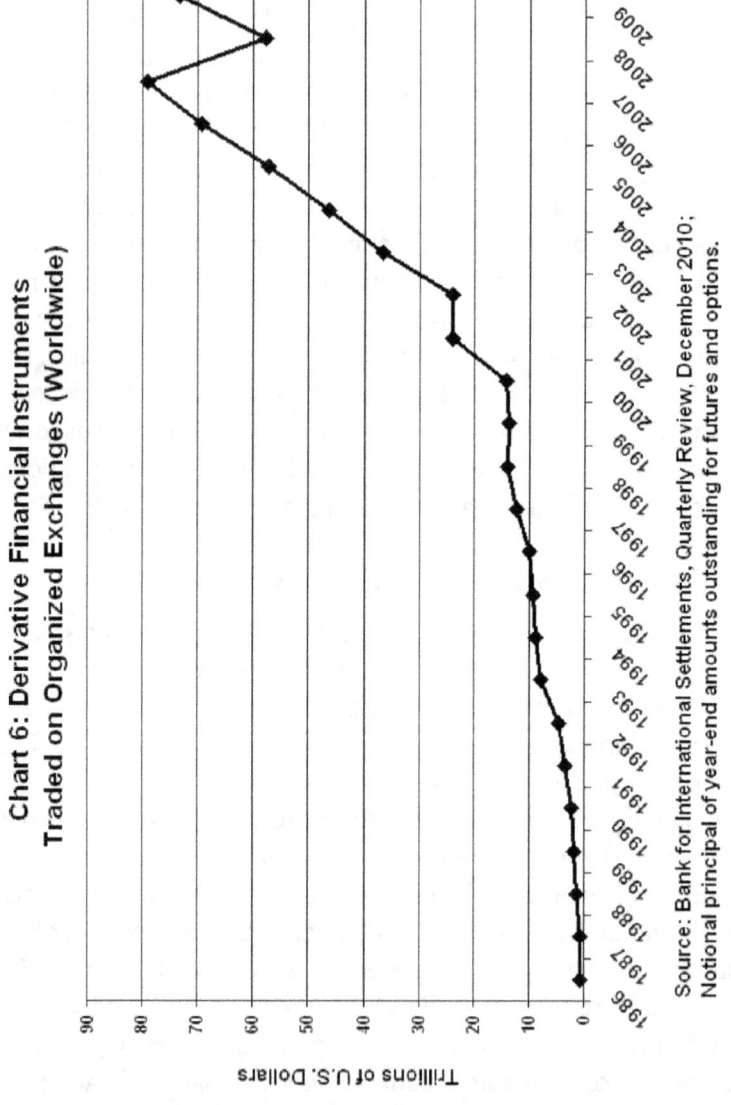

Chart 6: Derivative Financial Instruments
Traded on Organized Exchanges (Worldwide)

Source: Bank for International Settlements, Quarterly Review, December 2010;
Notional principal of year-end amounts outstanding for futures and options.

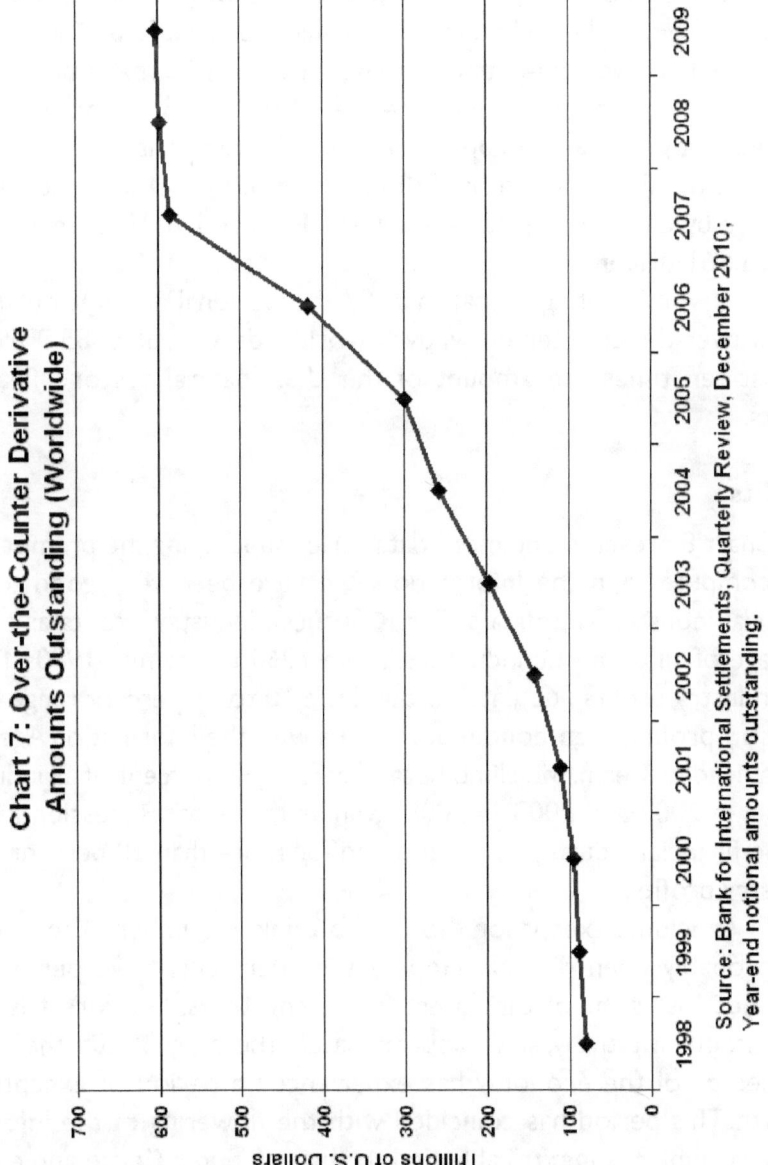

Chart 7: Over-the-Counter Derivative Amounts Outstanding (Worldwide)

Source: Bank for International Settlements, Quarterly Review, December 2010; Year-end notional amounts outstanding.

25

For derivative financial instruments traded on organized exchanges, the notional principal amount outstanding increased between 1998 and 2007—the decade before the bottom of the world's financial system fell out—from $14.0 trillion to $79.1 trillion, or by a factor of approximately 6. For over-the-counter derivatives, the notional amount outstanding increased during the same years from $80.3 trillion to $585.9 trillion, or by a factor of approximately 7. By comparison, the financial assets of the financial sector of the U.S. economy merely doubled—an increase by a factor of just 2—between 1998 and 2007, from $30 trillion to $61 trillion.

Also worth noting is that in 2007 the notional amount outstanding of over-the-counter derivatives worldwide was, at $585.9 trillion, almost ten times the amount of the U.S. financial sector's financial assets.

Profits

Chart 8 presents one more data series supporting the premise that the computer and the Information Age have been very good to the financial industry. The data series is financial industry profits as a percentage of all domestic industries. From 1960 to the mid-1980s, financial industry profits fluctuated around the 10 to 15 percent range of all industry profits. Then, contemporaneous with the Information Age getting a head of steam, the climb began, reaching 40 percent of all industry profits in 2002 and 2003. In 2008, even as the Great Recession kicked in, the financial industry still accounted for more than 20 percent of all industry profits.

To conclude, except for those who think in numbers, the chapter has probably been difficult. Hopefully, readers who have persevered have not lost sight of the forest for all the trees. The forest is simply this: quantitatively, since approximately the early 1980s, the financial sector of the economy has experienced a period of exceptional growth. This period has coincided with the flowering of the Information Age, which is inextricably tied to the computer. Cause and effect? You be the judge.

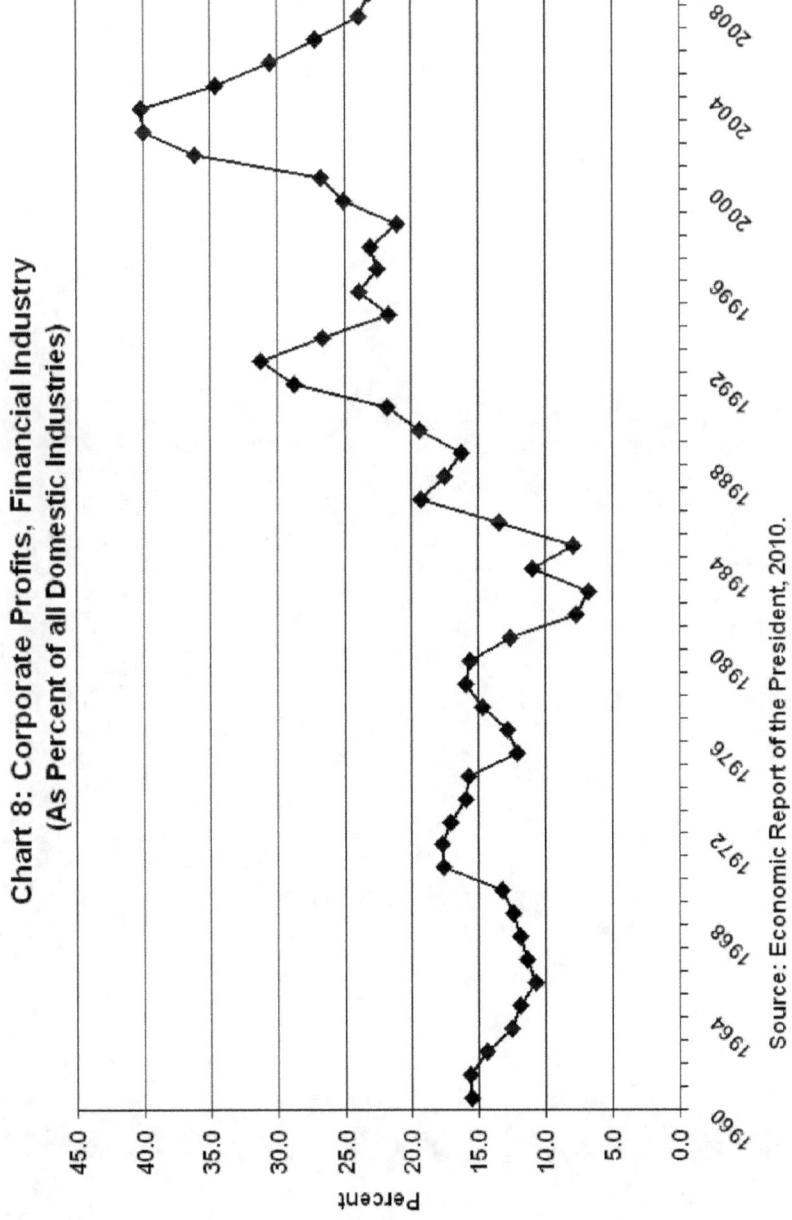

Chart 8: Corporate Profits, Financial Industry
(As Percent of all Domestic Industries)

Source: Economic Report of the President, 2010.

27

3

The Computer

What has been the computer's role in financialization? The basic answer is twofold. First, the computer increased exponentially the speeds at which financial information is spread and financial transactions are processed. Second, the computational power of the computer contributed to the appearance of new players in the financial marketplace, the growing complexity of that marketplace, and the development of a variety of opaque financial instruments, the more insidious of which involved multiple layers of financial assets.

Don't buy these assertions? Then read what Alan Greenspan had to say in a speech on banking supervision in 2000: "The speed of transactions and the growing complexities of these instruments have required federal and state examiners to focus supervision more on risk-management procedures than on actual portfolios."[1] If increasing speed and complexity were changing how banks were supervised, it seems safe to conclude that how banks operated, indeed the nature of the banking business, was also undergoing alteration. Maybe something even more profound was happening. Maybe economics itself was morphing into a new discipline: computernomics. Hang onto that thought in the pages and chapters ahead.

Few who remember the pre-computer age—roughly prior to the mid- to late 1970s—should dispute that the speed of information dissemination has accelerated dramatically over the last several decades. A sizeable subset of this information is financial in nature: stock prices, commodity prices, financial data of individuals, businesses, and governments, opinions on all of the aforementioned, and more. Not that all the information disseminated is accurate. Indeed, the amount of inaccurate, incomplete, or misleading information in cyberspace is a problem in its own right. But whether the financial information is good or bad, there is no shortage of it in the Information Age.

As for the processing of financial transactions, much of the work has most definitely been streamlined. For example, loan applications can be completed and approved with little in the way of physical exertion on the part of individuals: a few clicks on the computer and the necessary data are found, the application is formally made, and the approval accomplished. Or consider the legal contracts that create all manner of financial instruments. One does not start from scratch for each new addition to the world's total of financial assets. A template is called up, drafts and counter drafts are exchanged electronically, a few junior and mid-level legal worker bees spend a night—or a few nights—proofreading, and bingo, wealth has increased.

Increased speeds for information dissemination and the processing of transactions were just the beginning of the changes wrought by the computer in the financial arena. Once the computational power of this new machine was unleashed, human ingenuity—or perhaps more accurately, human perversity—took charge. The basic financial instruments—stocks and bonds—were joined by an increasing variety of complex brothers, sisters, cousins, and in-laws. An important component of this creative exuberance was a process known as securitization.

Securitization

The concept of securitization is fairly simple: discrete financial assets are pooled, and securities representing rights to income from the pool are sold to investors. Okay, securitization is generally not described in such an informal fashion. Here is a more formal effort: "Securitization is the creation and issuance of debt securities, or bonds, whose payments of principal and interest derive from cash flows generated by separate pools of assets."[2]

Another way to describe securitization is to consider two things that it is not. First, securitization is not a bank or other lender—that is, provider of credit—making a loan and keeping the loan on its books as an asset, and receiving the interest payments and the eventual repayment. Second, securitization is not a bank or other lender making a loan and then selling the loan to another institution that does nothing more than keeps the loan on its books as a discrete asset, receiving the interest payments and the eventual repayment.

Modern securitization first appeared in the mortgage field. In 1970, the Government National Mortgage Association, Ginnie Mae, began guaranteeing mortgage pass-through securities.[3] The pass-through refers to the passing through of mortgage principal and interest payments to investors. Ginnie Mae, an agency of the U.S. Government, was soon joined in securitization by Fannie Mae and Freddie Mac, private corporations sponsored by the U.S. Government. This federal government involvement in the creation and growth of mortgage pass-through securities, or simply mortgage-backed securities (MBS), arose from a policy goal of increasing the opportunities for home ownership. Securitization attracted both lenders and investors to the mortgage field, thus increasing the amount of funds available for mortgage lending.

The development of securitization since the creation of the first MBS in the 1970s is reflected in the proliferation of acronyms. CMOs— collateralized mortgage obligations—appeared in the early 1980s.[4] The CMO is to the MBS as complexity is to simplicity, as juggling multiple relationships is to monogamous marriage, as the existing tax code is to a no-exceptions flat rate tax, as the current health care system is to Marcus Welby, M.D. Investors in CMOs do not own the right to a simply calculated portion of the total payment stream from a pool of mortgages. Rather, they own the right to a payment stream that is the result of slicing and dicing the mortgage pool into classes, called tranches, with different degrees of risk. As time has gone on, the slicing and dicing have become ever more exuberant and the classes ever less understandable.

In the mid-1980s, securitization began reaching beyond mortgages and CMOs to other financial assets, the resulting acronym being ABS for asset-backed securities.[5] Financial assets securitized into ABSs include, but are not limited to, equipment leases, auto loans, student loans, and credit card receivables. And, of course, as the MBS spawned the CMO, the ABS spawned the CDO, or collateralized debt obligation, which provides investors with cash flow options based on the certainty—or risk—of payment streams created by slicing and dicing pools of non-mortgage financial assets into tranches.[6]

MBS, CMO, ABS, and CDO are by no means the only securitization acronyms. As the securitization concept has spread and variations in the basic structures appeared, keeping track of the terminology has become a considerable challenge.

How important has securitization become for the finance system? Between 2005 and 2007, just under half of the credit originated by financial institutions in the United States was securitized.[7] A December 2008 research report by analysts with Citigroup concluded that $8.7 trillion of global assets were funded through securitization.[8]

And what does securitization have to do with computers? Simply that securitization could not have achieved the importance it has without the computer. Forming asset pools, establishing different risk classes, keeping track of who issued what to whom, calculating monetary transfers, all involve the storage and manipulation of massive amounts of data. One estimate is that a typical CDO has 30,000 pages of documentation.[9] Business schools and law schools do not graduate enough bodies to manually keep track of securitization's paper avalanche. Without the computer, securitization would not exist.

Derivatives

In one form or another, derivatives have existed for a good part of human commercial history. But in the Information Age they have moved from the corners of finance to center stage. They have been major beneficiaries of the computer's speed and computational power. In Chapter 2, derivatives were also called not-quite financial assets. This description was used because derivatives are generally not included in the Federal Reserve's Flow of Funds as debt or financial assets. In the world beyond the Fed's marble halls, however, derivatives are often described as—or maybe better, confused with—financial assets. The confusion likely creeps into discussions and mentions of derivatives in these chapters.

Derivatives are financial contracts whose values are "derived" from the prices of something else: tangible commodities; full-fledged financial assets; intangible indexes, conditions, or, well, you name it. Derivatives based on tangible assets—crops or livestock, for example—have a long history, a history that began well before the onset of the Information Age. Derivatives based on financial assets or intangibles of some sort are a much more recent innovation, an innovation in which the computer played, and plays, a leading role.

Major categories of derivatives are futures, options, and swaps. Futures are agreements to buy or sell something at a particular price on a specified future date. Options are agreements giving the right, but not the obligation, to buy or sell something at a particular price. Usually, a date or period of time is specified. Swaps involve the exchanging of one obligation for another, and the subject matter is limited only by human imagination. Interest rates and currencies are common subjects of swaps. Frequently, fixed and variable payment obligations are exchanged. Altering risk exposures is a major motivator for swap transactions. Indeed, shifting risks—usually to financial institutions that are willing, for a fee, to bear them—is a prime reason for much of the derivatives business.

This shifting of risks can be viewed as a form of insurance. A cautionary note about the derivatives-insurance comparison is warranted, however. Differences exist between the two, perhaps the most significant being that insurance costs are usually based on actuarial principles while the pricing and payoffs of derivatives are the province of financial modeling, arbitrage, and yes, guesswork.

Derivatives may be sold and traded on or off exchanges. On-exchange transactions eliminate or substantially reduce counterparty risk, which is the risk that one of the parties will not be able to fulfill its obligations under the derivative contract. The exchange bears the counterparty risk, and an adequately financed and operated exchange should be able to bear most instances of counterparty failure. On-exchange transactions also are more transparent and provide those responsible for oversight—ultimately a governmental authority—a clearer picture of market size, direction, and risk than do off-exchange transactions. Unfortunately for both counterparty risk and oversight, however, the largest growth in financial derivatives has been off exchanges (see Chapter 2).

Financial engineering ingenuity has produced many variations and combinations of the basic derivative categories, one very notable example being the infamous credit default swap (CDS) that contributed so much to the financial difficulties that exploded in 2007-08. CDSs can be viewed as a form of insurance, and indeed insurance—the attempt to control risks—is, as noted several paragraphs ago, a key aspect of derivatives in general. In a simple example of insurance, a lender might want to buy protection against a borrower's default. The seller of that protection—that insurance—could be a third party. That sounds innocuous enough. After all, a lender certainly has an interest—an insurable interest—in the funds that have been advanced. If the borrower were unable to repay the loan, the insurance would partially or fully offset the lender's loss.

But some analysts of the situation say "Not so fast." Henry Hu was recruited by Securities and Exchange Commission Chairman Mary Schapiro in 2009 to head a new SEC division, the Division of Risk, Strategy and Financial Innovation. Mr. Hu had developed a theory about derivative use in financial markets, the "empty creditor" theory.[10] A lender, such as a bank, that uses a derivative, such as a CDS, to eliminate any loss if the borrower goes bankrupt becomes an "empty creditor." The lender's concern about the borrower's survival is lower, perhaps considerably lower, than in the case in which the lender stands to lose financially if the borrower defaults. If too many lenders practice "empty crediting," financial markets might become less stable. An important cautionary component of the markets loses some of its potency.

In an April 2009 article in The Wall Street Journal, Mr. Hu applied an "empty creditor" analysis to one of the most significant events of the financial meltdown, the downfall of AIG.[11] In Mr. Hu's analysis, investment bank Goldman Sachs' use of CDSs might have made it an "empty creditor" of AIG. Goldman Sachs apparently lent at least $7 billion to AIG. To protect itself, Goldman bought CDSs that would pay off if AIG defaulted on its debt. As AIG's troubles became evident, Goldman, apparently confident that it was adequately protected by the CDSs, did not show much inclination to work with its debtor, AIG. Instead, it aggressively sought increased collateral from AIG, a stance that increased the tenuousness of the latter's predicament. Mr. Hu's implication is that if Goldman had not had the CDS protection, it would have been more willing to help AIG work through the situation.

But the "empty creditor" situation is just the beginning of the problems with CDSs. In a sense, "empty creditor" is the plain vanilla situation: a lender protects itself by buying insurance against the borrower's default. What if unrelated third parties are buying the insurance?

In the fields of life and property insurance, it is generally necessary to have an insurable interest in a person or property in order to obtain insurance on that person or property. Perhaps the best example is found in life insurance. Purchasing life insurance on an individual with whom one has a little or no connection is in most instances not allowed.[12] The theory is that the would-be purchaser has no interest in the insured's continued existence but would profit from the insured's ceasing to exist. Moral hazard is a polite way to describe the situation that would be created. Motivation to commit mayhem might be another way.

Such a general requirement for an insurable interest was *not* an essential element of the CDS market that developed in the late 1990s and grew exponentially in the early years of the new century. The buyer of a CDS was not required to have an interest in the underlying instrument, which might be a debt obligation, a credit exposure, a security of some sort, or whatever. The buyer of a CDS was also not required to have any connection with the parties to the underlying instrument. Party A could make a loan to Party B, and unrelated Party C could buy a CDS from Party D. If Party B defaulted on the loan from Party A, Party D would pay off the CDS to Party C. A more succinct way to put the matter is that Party C could make a bet with Party D that Party B would default to Party A. A CDS in which the purchaser is not required to have an interest in or connection with the underlying financial instrument is often called a naked CDS.

Why would Party C (the CDS purchaser) and Party D (the CDS seller) make such a bet? One motivation for the CDS seller is simply to receive income. The seller likely has concluded that the chance of default on the underlying financial instrument is remote. Consequently, the CDS seller sees income with little risk. From the viewpoint of the CDS purchaser, a motivation might be to have protection from a fall in value of a financial instrument or instruments related to or correlated with the underlying financial instrument. Or the CDS purchaser's motivation might be more speculative: a bet that corporation X or country Y is heading for financial trouble.

A final point on derivatives is that they create leverage, that is, debt or potential debt. This point is sufficiently significant that a later chapter on fractional reserve banking delves into it at greater length. Suffice for the moment to note that derivative contracts are, in the succinct words of The Economist, "sealed with initial payments that are a small fraction of the potential gain or loss."[13]

And the computer's role in derivatives? As with securitization, the modern derivative is a creature of the computer. The massive requirements for data storage, exchange, and manipulation in creating and trading today's derivatives could not be met without that tool.

Modeling

No, this section is not about attractive women and men sashaying down a runway—although it is about something that can be just as ephemeral and pretentious. In the worlds of finance and economics, modeling refers to attempts at representing the "real" world with mathematical models. A modest goal of the effort is insight into the portion of the "real" world that is the subject of the model. The modest goal, however, can very easily slide down the proverbial slippery slope to a specific prediction, if not of a single outcome at least of a well-defined range of outcomes.

Modeling has become ubiquitous in finance and economics. And in practically all cases it requires the computer. Modeling entails the identification of multiple relationships, the isolation and quantification of causes and effects, the input and manipulation of often vast amounts of data. Financial institutions use modeling to develop and operate investment, trading, hedging, and speculation strategies. Financial industry overseers and observers use modeling to reach conclusions about the safety and soundness of individual institutions and about the condition of the overall financial system or parts thereof. A subset of financial industry entrepreneurs do little more than develop and sell models.

Risk is the direct or indirect target of many modeling efforts. What is the current level of risk of a trade, position, or institution, current often not being a leisurely time span but an hour ago, right now, or an hour hence? How would the level of risk change if such-and-such happened?

But as complex as some of them are, models provide only an incomplete view of the "real" world. Pertinent variables escape identification. Relationships are murkier in reality than in the precise world of algorithms. Data are incomplete. Time period selection is inappropriate—too short, too long, or just plain irrelevant to the problem at hand. And then there is the "Black Swan," the unexpected event lurking in the tail of the probabilistic bell-shaped curve that is inherent in a large number of modeling efforts.

Many individual models are versions of a basic form. One of the basic forms is the Black-Scholes option pricing model, which was developed in the 1970s and is still going strong. Today, it is a mainstay of attempts to value derivatives. Another form is value-at-risk, or VAR. Its development is attributed to work at JPMorgan in the late 1980s and early 1990s.[14] VAR models are used by financial institutions to quantify, often in a single number, the risk of loss in a portfolio of assets. VAR results are relied upon by regulators in determining bank capital requirements. More recently, stress testing has become popular in the financial industry. Stress testing involves envisioning scenarios, such as rise in interest rates to a certain percentage or a fall in equity prices to a specified level, and calculating what the results would be for a specific institution. As one of the responses to the financial crises of 2007-2009, stress testing by large U.S. banking organizations was mandated by federal banking regulators in the spring of 2009.[15]

An example of the uncertainty of the modeling business was noted in an early 2010 report in *The Economist*.[16] Using its own model, Morgan Stanley arrived at a VAR figure of $115 million for the first quarter of 2009. But if Goldman Sach's method had been applied to Morgan Stanley, the latter's VAR would have been $158 million.

A succinct way to characterize the dangers inherent in relying too much on modeling is the old adage, "garbage in, garbage out." In the Information Age, a tremendous amount of garbage can be input. All too often, the output is still garbage.

Dark Money and Shadow Banking

Another component of financialization is the rise of "dark money." The term is neither formal nor precise. A general, blurry, exclusionary definition is that dark money is money not readily transparent to regulatory authorities, financial markets, and the general public. Another definitional element could be that dark money is not readily available to the general public. A contrast might be illustrative. Mutual funds are not dark money. Mutual funds are sold to the general public, are subject to a fairly comprehensive regulatory regime, and maintain public financial records. Hedge funds are dark money. Hedge funds are by and large not sold to the general public, are subject to minimal oversight by government regulators, and do not provide easy access to their full financial condition.

Dark money and shadow banking—the latter a more widely used term introduced in the preceding chapter—refer to overlapping but not identical things. Under one definition, shadow banking refers to financial intermediaries that perform maturity, credit, and liquidity transformations but do not have access to central bank liquidity or public sector credit guarantees.[17] In other words, shadow banks are outside the traditional banking system. In contrast, dark money can be found in both the shadow banking and traditional banking systems.

Three leading examples of dark money are hedge funds, private equity funds, and proprietary trading. Hedge funds come in assorted sizes, have assorted purposes, and are subject to not a lot of regulation. Generally, hedge funds are open to only a narrow range of investors. Having lots of assets is the usual way to qualify as a hedge fund investor. Each hedge fund designs and pursues a particular strategy but as a group their investments range the full gamut of equity shares, debt instruments, and commodities. Hedge funds usually are active traders of their investments. And as the term implies, hedging risk can be a central focus. The hedging is accomplished with derivatives and through trading strategies, such as short selling. Aggressive hedging, however, trods a narrow path between increasing and reducing risk. Lastly, in addition to money from their investors, hedge funds also borrow considerable amounts. In other words, they are leveraged, often highly leveraged.

Private equity funds make investments that are generally less liquid than the investments of hedge funds. Often the investments are not in publicly traded instruments or companies, and are relatively illiquid. A common private equity investment is in a small company starting up or seeking to expand. Venture capital is a term describing such an investment. Another common private equity investment is in a company that is a likely target, perhaps after a strengthening or revamping of management, of a merger or acquisition. Like hedge funds, private equity funds often operate with considerable leverage.

Proprietary trading refers to an institution's use of its own funds—rather than funds it holds for its customers—to trade stocks, bonds, currencies, commodities, and other financial instruments. The goal is to make profits.

Most large banks in the United States have trading desks. They may also be involved with hedge funds and private equity funds. In early 2010, The Wall Street Journal took note of trading and fund activities of six large U.S. banks.[18] Bank of America had both a proprietary trading unit and a private equity business. Citicorp engaged in proprietary trading and had in-house private equity, real estate, and hedge funds. Goldman Sachs, which before 2008 had been an investment bank and not a commercial bank, received approximately 10 percent of its revenues from proprietary trading. It had both private equity investments and hedge funds. JPMorgan Chase & Co. engaged in proprietary trading and had both a private equity business and a hedge fund unit. Morgan Stanley, another investment bank turned commercial bank, received somewhat under 5 percent of its revenues from hedge fund activities and proprietary trading. Only Wells Fargo appeared barely involved in dark money activities.

A crucial element of dark money, an element that contributes to its lack of transparency to regulators, the public, and financial markets themselves, is its off-exchange or over-the-counter locus. Financial assets that do not change hands on public exchanges such as the New York Stock Exchange leave a much more uncertain valuation trail than do exchange-traded assets. And it is not only exotic forms of derivatives, such as credit default swaps, that are found in off-exchange trading. Financial assets in off-exchange trading can include U.S. Government and agency bonds, municipal and corporate bonds, asset-backed and mortgage securities, and collateralized debt obligations. Indeed, one analysis concluded that for the years 2001 through 2006, less than half of all securities trades were on exchanges with easily available price information.[19] In the article presenting this analysis, *The Wall Street Journal* headlined that U.S. investors had entered an "Age of Murky Pricing."

And again, the role of the computer? Simply that absent the computer, the data storage, data manipulation, and data communication capacities necessary to support hedge funds, private equity funds, proprietary trading, and the other aspects of dark money would not exist.

* * *

4

Capitalism on Steroids

Students in introductory economics courses are confronted with a number of unfamiliar topics. Most of those topics—supply and demand curves, for example—are likely to be presented in a serious, solemn manner by the usually junior faculty members burdened with bringing the dismal science to their often less-than-enthusiastic charges. But two topics can sometimes rouse instructors from their lethargy, even prompting a few to use terms of awe, wonderment, and mystery. The two topics are compound interest and fractional reserve banking.

The two topics have a similarity: they seem to describe the creation of something from nothing, or at least from very little. Compound interest presents the easier intellectual challenge. It is reducible to simple formulas, perhaps the most common of which is $FV = PV(1+i)^n$, where FV is the future value of the present value PV on which an interest rate i accrues for n periods. In other words, just leave a sum in an interest-bearing savings account or comparable investment long enough and it will get really large.

Fractional reserve banking is somewhat more involved. It is also somewhat removed from the individual, pertaining to broader matters: the banking system, macroeconomics, capitalism, the creation of money. The last factor—the creation of money—is what the Information Age has brought to the forefront. The computer has combined with fractional reserve banking to make money creation a very simple matter, at least for those advantageously located. In turn, and not yet fully appreciated, the resulting money creation machine is bringing fundamental changes to the banking system, macroeconomics, and yes, capitalism itself. Indeed, in discussions on the financialization of the recent past, and particularly of the first years of the 21st Century, the phrase "capitalism on steroids" sometimes pops up. The phrase is appropriate.

The Model

The simplistic model of the fractional reserve banking system begins with a fact: the amount of printed money in circulation—in the United States, the 1, 2, 5, 10, 20, 50, 100, and so on dollar bills—is only a small fraction of the total money in use. Most of the money in use is created when banks and other financial institutions make loans. The standard way of explaining money creation under a fractional reserve banking system is to begin with money being put into a bank. Say an individual deposits $1,000 into a bank checking account. The bank is required to keep only a portion of that actually on hand, "actually on hand" usually meaning in the bank itself or in an account with a central authority such as the Federal Reserve System in the United States. The requirement of how much the bank has to keep "actually on hand" is set by law and is commonly called the bank's required reserve. The current reserve requirement for banks in the United States is, basically, 10 percent of net transaction accounts, which are checking and similar accounts.

For a required reserve ratio of 10 percent, the bank has to keep $100 of the $1,000 deposit as reserve. That leaves the bank free to make a loan of the remaining $900. Thus the initial deposit of $1,000 has led to the creation of an additional $900. Described from another perspective, the nation's supply of money—the money supply—has increased by $900.

What becomes of the $900 in new money? The borrower might just park it temporarily in his or her checking account. Or the borrower might convert the $900 into something tangible: a television, or raw materials for the making of a product. The seller of the television or raw materials might then deposit the $900 in his or her checking account. In either case, the $900 is back in a checking account in a bank and can thus support another round of money creation. The bank holding the account—it might actually be the same bank as holds the first $1,000 deposit—can loan 90 percent of the $900, or $810, keeping the remaining $90 as its required 10 percent reserve. The total money now created—the total increase in the money supply—is $1,710 ($900 plus $810).

If this process is taken through ten steps—admittedly, a somewhat unrealistic exercise—the total amount on deposit is increased from $1,000 to $6,513.22 (Table 1). Thus in a ten-step model, the original $1,000 is supporting an increase in the money supply of $5,513.22, or 551 percent. The theoretical maximum amount of money that an initial deposit could become can be calculated by a formula, the money multiplier formula: $m = 1/R$ where m is the money multiplier and R is the reserve ratio. A reserve ratio of 10 percent, or 1/10 or 0.10, results in $m = 10$. Thus an initial deposit of $1,000 can theoretically become $10,000, an increase of 900 percent.

Table 1. Increase in Bank Deposits (and Money Supply) through Ten Steps ($1,000 Initial Deposit and 10% Required Reserve Ratio)		
Step Amounted Deposited	Lent by Banks	Reserved
1.	$ 1000.00	$ 900.00	$ 100.00
2.	900.00	810.00	90.00
3.	810.00	729.00	81.00
4.	729.00	656.10	72.90
5.	656.10	590.49	65.61
6.	590.49	531.44	59.05
7.	531.44	478.30	53.14
8.	478.30	430.47	47.83
9.	430.47	387.42	43.05
10.	387.42	348.68	38.74
Total Amount Deposited:	Total Increase in Bank Lending:	Total Increase in Bank Reserves:
$6513.22	$5861.90	$651.32

Increase in money supply: $5,513.22 ($6,513.22 total amount deposited minus $1,000 initial deposit).

But, the skeptic asks, his or her head swimming a little at this point, what happens when a depositor withdraws his or her deposit? Doesn't the loan based on that deposit have to be called in? Perhaps such would be the case for a very, very small bank. But banks aren't very, very small. They are large, some very, very large. The one deposit and one loan are only two transactions of thousands, tens of thousands, hundreds of thousands that the bank has on its books at any one time. The determination of lending capacity and reserves is made in the aggregate, taking into account all of the deposits and other funds of various types held by the bank. And the mix is in constant motion. As one depositor is withdrawing $1,000, another individual is becoming a depositor by putting money in.

Not persuaded, the skeptic persists. What if, in the aggregate, more deposits go out than come in? And what if this occurs very quickly, so there isn't time to wind down the outstanding loans? In other words, what if there is a run on the bank? The short answer is, there's trouble, possibly a whole lot of trouble. But the more realistic answer is that such events are infrequent, very infrequent. And when such events have occurred, governments have often teamed with bankers to patch the system. This is not to say that there hasn't been pain. There has been, sometimes lots of it. But, to date, there has always been a recovery. Knock on wood.

Although an explanation of the phenomenon usually begins with a deposit in a bank, the term "fractional reserve banking" is commonly used in a broader sense. The broader sense does not focus on the source of funds—in the model just described, a deposit—but on the money creation aspect. A deposit in a bank is a liability of the bank. The amount by which a bank's assets exceed its liabilities is a bank's equity or capital. Both a bank's liabilities and its capital support money creation. Reserve requirements—which may also go by the terms liquidity requirements or liquidity ratios—limit money creation from liabilities, at least those liabilities enumerated in the requirements. Capital requirements limit money creation from capital, or the excess of assets over liabilities. Leverage requirements—the amount of capital or assets to back debt—can also enter the picture.

Real world reserve and capital requirements get pretty detailed, with attempts at precise definitions of various types of assets and capital and myriad exceptions and qualifications abounding. In addition, the business of setting requirements has become international, a focus of the Basel Committee on Banking Supervision, headquartered in Basel, Switzerland. The Committee is an entity of the Bank for International Settlements (BIS) and provides a forum for regular cooperation on bank supervision matters. Capital adequacy standards have been the best known of those matters. The Committee develops standards, which are implemented in each country by that country's banking authorities. The central banks of 56 nations are the membership of the BIS, and 27 of those nations are members of the Committee on Banking Supervision.

The Committee first pronounced capital standards in 1988. A major revision, known as Basel II, was issued in 2004. In December 2010, Basel III arrived with details of global regulatory standards for capital adequacy, liquidity, and leverage. Much of Basel III was a response to the financial crisis that surfaced in 2007-08. Basel III provides for relatively long implementation periods. For example, initial implementation for the capital standards is 2013. Complicating the matter in the United States is that the major financial reform law enacted in the summer of 2010, the Dodd-Frank Wall Street Reform and Consumer Protection Act, also contains provisions dealing with capital adequacy and related matters. Dodd-Frank is discussed in the final chapter of this book.

Fortunately, plenty of lawyers and accountants are around to handle the details that make fractional reserve banking work. The broad point is that fractional reserve banking has been fundamental to banking and finance since at least the 18th Century. The historian Niall Ferguson traces fractional reserve banking to the Swedish Riksbank, which was founded in 1656.[1] Other historians refer, often rather vaguely, to the goldsmiths of Elizabethan times. The goldsmiths' business was to hold the gold of others for safekeeping. When gold was left with a goldsmith, he gave the owner a receipt. These gold receipts came to be accepted as money, as a means to purchase goods and services from others. At some point, goldsmiths began issuing more gold receipts than they had gold on deposit. The gold receipts morphed into banknotes, and the issuance of banknotes to someone who had not deposited gold was—cue the music—the lending of money.

Whatever the murky origins, fractional reserve banking appears to have been firmly established in the major commercial centers of Europe—and the new United States—by the late 18th Century. As a consequence, lending, or the advancing of credit, had become not just a fundamental component of banking and finance; credit provided the fuel for the expansion of commerce and the developing industrial age. The economic advances of the last several centuries flowed from credit, and were thus a product of fractional reserve banking.

Alternatives

Fractional reserve banking is accompanied by a lot of baggage: capital ratios, liquidity ratios, reserve ratios, money multipliers, money supply definitions, and much more. Indeed, study of the baggage occupies a goodly portion of an economic major's time, so much so that basic questions often are given short shrift. One basic question: Was—is—fractional reserve banking inevitable?

As beneficial as most mainstream economists probably think it has been, fractional reserve banking is not without its critics. One avenue of criticism concerns the periods of instability and economic loss. Whether one views these periods as frequent or only occasional, the fact is that they occur. And in almost all instances they have been preceded by a time of exuberant lending, of too much credit. In other words, fractional reserve banking may be good, but it can also be bad.

Efforts over the decades and centuries to control the negative consequences of fractional reserve banking have usually taken the form of increased government oversight. Initially, the amount of reserves was something a bank decided itself, listening to its private voice of prudence. When these voices proved flawed, reserve requirements were imposed by the state. Other government initiatives have been central banking systems—the Federal Reserve System being the United States' version—and deposit insurance.

But to the consternation of those who view economics and governance as steady state matters, the demand for changes that new crises precipitate can be troubling, in large measure because the demands usually are in the direction of more oversight, ultimately by government. Thus the siren call of an unchangeable foundation for banking and finance beckons a few critics of fractional reserve banking. The most direct alternative to fractional reserve banking is full reserve banking, which is how some banks operated in pre-fractional reserve times. In full reserve banking, there would be no lending of depositors' funds and thus no money creation by the banks. There would also be, it is argued, little danger of bank runs because the full amount of each depositor's funds is always available for withdrawal.

But consideration of alternatives to fractional reserve banking is largely confined to backwaters of the economics profession and to theorists on the fringes of political thought. Fractional reserve banking is just too embedded in modern economies to attract serious critical scrutiny. Perhaps someday a combination of financial instability, anti-central bank feeling, antagonism to Wall Street, oddities such as gold standard fervor, and yes, technology run amok will precipitate that scrutiny, but the day does not seem imminent.

Comes the Computer

Wait, did you say technology run amok? Isn't that a thesis of this very book? Well, now that you mention it. . . . So what about the confluence of fractional reserve banking and the Information Age?

The reader probably realizes that the model of fractional reserve banking presented earlier in the chapter is a simplification—a gross simplification, really—of a very complex money creation system. Indeed, using a money multiplier approach on aggregate banking industry data in order to determine the relationship between total bank credit and some hypothetical starting point from which a money creation process began, well, the effort quickly becomes unappealing. In short, reality is a lot messier than theory.

Reality also changes. The reality that governed the world of which fractional reserve banking was a fundamental part is giving way. The reality of this fading world was tangibility. Banking and finance served an economic system dominated by the production, distribution, and acquisition of goods. In the evolving world, the new world, the ephemeral is displacing the tangible as the focus of banking and finance. In the ephemeral world, multiple layers of intangible financial assets are where the action is. And the computer is the tool making this ephemeral world possible.

One justification for fractional reserve banking is the expansion of the money supply to meet the needs of commerce, of the production, distribution, and acquisition of goods. But what if more than the needs are met? What if the things being met are no more than desires?

Return for a moment to the chart detailing the increase in bank deposits and money supply. An unstated assumption of the model is that most of the money lent—the middle column labeled "Lent by Banks"—has an impact on substantive economic activity. Goods are produced, services closely related to goods are rendered. A money multiplier of 10 results in a tenfold—900 percent—increase in both the money supply AND real economic activity.

But in Information Age finance, maybe the money supply increase consistently outstrips the increase in real economic activity.

Money Supply

The term "money supply" has been bandied about rather haphazardly thus far in this work. It's time for a harder look at the animal. Don't worry, it won't take long.

In the United States, the Federal Reserve issues weekly statistics on the money stock measures M1 and M2. Briefly, M1 consists of the most liquid forms of money, namely currency and checkable deposits. M2 includes M1 plus primarily household holdings of savings deposits, small time deposits, and retail money market mutual funds. Until 2006 the Fed also had an M3 monetary aggregate that included, among other items, large-denomination time deposits and institutional money market mutual funds. The Fed still keeps track of the components but not of their aggregation as M3.

M1 and M2 seem to serve the Federal Reserve's needs for tracking the most immediate types of money. But they certainly do not appear to reflect the status of other types or forms of money. The components of the abandoned M3—large-denomination time deposits, institutional money market mutual funds, and a few other items—continue to be money in some context.

What is money anyway? At one end of a money spectrum is a medium of immediate or almost immediate exchange, such as M1 and M2. At the other end? That end is a little less clear. Perhaps wealth is an answer. One commonality along the spectrum is information. The money spectrum is a spectrum of information, information on values of a range of assets.

Financial assets are money. Financial assets differ in the ease and quickness with which the different types can be reduced to an immediate medium of exchange. But ultimately, the different types—stocks, bonds, whatever—are all money. And to the extent that wealth is composed of financial assets, wealth is money.[2]

Credit is also money. Credit can be used to produce goods and related services. Unfortunately, credit can also be used to produce more credit. Margin is a form of credit, or more accurately, margin produces credit. Buying or investing in a financial asset on margin means putting up only a portion of the price of the asset. The remainder of the price is a loan to the buyer.

So currency, checkable deposits, savings deposits, small time deposits, large-denomination time deposits, retail and institutional money market mutual funds, corporate equities, bonds, credit as a result of lending, credit as a result of margin, financial assets created through the magic of financial engineering—they all equal money. At least in a very broad view of the matter.

Bottom Line

The bottom line: what an appropriate term to sum up a discussion of a topic in finance. The bottom line is that, broadly defined, money includes all types of financial assets. In the Industrial Age, the connection between financial assets on one hand and goods and related services on the other was fairly direct. Fractional reserve banking created money, but the money quickly became goods and related services. There was an ill-defined limit on how much money could be created, ill-defined but still a limit. In the Information Age, fractional reserve banking still creates money, only a lot more of it. The ill-defined limit has taken a giant step toward the horizon. Financial assets have taken on a life of their own. They don't reproduce slowly and in a controlled fashion. They reproduce by a much more prolific process, a process that is akin to cloning. The connection between financial assets and real goods and services is no longer short and direct. It can be long, meandering, and inconclusive.

In short, the Information Age has combined with fractional reserve banking to produce capitalism on steroids, or perhaps more accurately, capitalism run amok.

*** *

5

Patents and Finance, Say What?

Patents?! Why is the topic of patents in a tome on the financial melt-down of 2007-2009? Aren't patents about gadgets and the like?

With apologies to the late Johnny Carson, think again credit-default-swap breath.

No, patents did not cause the financial meltdown. But patents and the patent system provide evidence about two relevant matters. The first is the increasing complexity of the financial world. The second, and more troubling, is the apparent lack of understanding that the Information Age and its tool, the computer, are presenting fundamental challenges to many Industrial Age concepts. One of those concepts is intellectual property, particularly patents. Participants in the patent sys-tem—the U.S. Patent Office, courts, policymakers, industries, inventors, innovators—have for the most part attempted to fit the new world into the existing system. Perhaps nowhere has this attempt been more strained than with finance and the financial industry.

Patents, a Primer

Patents go back a long way. In England, patents were granted by the Crown as early as the 15th Century.[1] By 1787, patents were sufficiently established to be explicitly recognized in the new U.S. Constitution. Among the powers given to Congress in Article I, Section 8, was the power "To promote the progress of science and the useful arts, by securing for limited times to authors and inventors the exclusive right to their respective writings and discoveries."

The first U.S. Patent Act was passed shortly thereafter, in 1790. It permit-ted patents upon "any useful art, manufacture, engine, machine, or device, or any improvement therein not before known or used."[2] The list of what was patentable was changed just three years later, in the Patent Act of 1793. Under the 1793 Act, a patent could be granted for "any new and useful art, machine, manufacture or composition of matter," or improvement thereof.[3] This description of what was patentable remained unchanged for more than 150 years. In 1952, the word "process" replaced "art," a substitution that some have found significant but that the U.S. Supreme Court, for one, has appeared to view as of no great import.[4] The 1952 language has not been changed. Thus the current list of what is patentable—"any new and useful process, machine, manufacture, or composition of matter," or improvements thereof [5]—has in essence existed for over 200 years, with just the probably slight modification of "process" replacing "art" in 1952.

Until the last decades of the 20th Century, tangibility was an unstated characteristic of the vast majority of patents. Most patents were for tangible things, or things with a close relationship to tangible things. After all, the Industrial Age was all about tangible stuff. Three of the patent categories—machine, manufacture, and composition of matter—were overtly tangible. For patents on inventions and discoveries in the fourth category—"art," which was morphed in 1952 to "process"—a nexus to one of the tangible categories was implicitly or explicitly present. In the words of one authority, "the unpatentability of processes not involving manufactures, machines, or compositions of matter has been firmly embedded in the statute since the time of the Patent Act of 1793."[6] Similarly, "there is no evidence that patents were granted under the 1793 Act on methods of organizing human activity not involving manufactures, machines or the creation of compositions of matter."[7]

Despite the explicit patent categories in the law, and maybe due in part to the pervasiveness of tangibility in Industrial Age inventions and discoveries, and certainly due in part to the exuberance of the patent attorneys and practitioners, a feeling of no limits crept into the views of some in the patent field. This view was captured in the phrase "anything under the sun that is made by man." The phrase appeared in Congressional Committee Reports accompanying the 1952 Patent Act and was cited with apparent approval by the Supreme Court in a 1980 decision, *Diamond v. Chakrabarty.*[8]

But as the Court noted in the very same case, there were limits. Citing previous decisions dating back to 1853, the Court said that laws of nature, physical phenomena, and abstract ideas had been held not patentable. As theoretical examples, the Court said that Einstein could not have patented $E = mc^2$, nor Newton the law of gravity.

Thus at the dawn of the Information Age, the U.S. patent system was a source of comfort and stability. Its legal underpinnings and structure had remained largely unchanged for almost two centuries. Its reach extended to almost every nook and cranny of the economy, in large measure because the Industrial Age economy was an edifice of predominately tangible things. Its limits were fairly well established at the line where tangible creations by humans gave way to mere statements and descriptions of laws of nature, physical phenomena, and abstract ideas.

And then came the computer.

Patents and the Information Age

As the computer in its various manifestations began spreading its tentacles across the economy in the 1960s, '70s, and '80s, computer-related patent applications reflected the changing world. The applications fell into three groups: hardware, software, and, for want of a better term, business methods.

The hardware applications presented little difficulty. Computers were machines, and computer hardware was tangible. Hardware applications easily fit into the existing structure for determining patentability.

Software, however, was a problem. Software alone was obviously not a machine. But without software, computers, which were machines, performed no functions. They were just collections of tangible components. In 1968, the Patent Office adopted guidelines under which a computer program—software—was not patentable. But the Patent Office also indicated that a programmed computer could be a component of a patentable process if combined with unobvious elements to produce a physical result.[9] The federal court with prime jurisdiction over patent questions at the time—the Court of Customs and Patent Appeals—quickly began picking away at the Patent Office's absolute position of no patents for stand-alone software. The Supreme Court eventually entered the fray with several less-than-clear decisions.[10] The result seemed to be that a mathematical algorithm standing alone was not patentable but might be when part of a system including some ill-defined amount of hardware. The courts appeared to go out of their way to avoid the broad-brush term "software" itself, and to avoid the term that was becoming common: software patents.

But the uncertainty about what was and was not patentable was just gathering steam. The computer put a gargantuan amount of analyzing capability into human hands, and humans began enthusiastically applying that capability in many divergent directions, one of them being finance. The objects of many of these analytical efforts lacked the dominating tangibility that had characterized Industrial Age patentability. In some instances, the object might be an exotic new financial instrument, such as a credit default swap. In this case, the object was an intangible. In other instances, the object might be how to perform an activity involving an intangible, such as how to manage a mutual fund. What was common about these intangible products and the intangible management of them was a false certainty created by the computer. If something intangible could be reduced to flow charts, detailed descriptions, and seemingly precise parameters, it was no longer intangible, right?

How might such intangibles fit into existing legal structures? Why, by golly, they might be processes and thus patentable under the patent laws! That "process" and its antecedent "art" had historically been defined rather narrowly under the patent laws was just a small hurdle. These new intangibles were for sure business methods, and thus processes, and thus patentable! Onwards and upwards!

In 1998, the floodgates opened for this line of thought, and for what many were now calling business methods patents. In that year, the Court of Appeals for the Federal Circuit—the successor to the Court of Customs and Patent Appeals[11]—handed down *State Sreet Bank & Trust Company v. Signature Financial Group*.[12] Signature and State Street were both in the financial services business. More precisely, the Federal Circuit said that both were in the business of acting "as custodians and accounting agents for multi-tiered partnership fund financial services." More colloquially, the Federal Circuit described Signature as an administrator and accounting agent for mutual funds.

Signature had developed and patented a data processing system with the proprietary name Hub and Spoke. The system facilitated a structure whereby mutual funds—the Spokes—pooled their assets in an investment portfolio—the Hub—organized as a partnership. This investment configuration provided the administrator of a mutual fund with the combination of economies of scale in administering investments and the tax advantages of a partnership. State Street first tried to license Signature's system. When negotiations floundered, State Street went to court, contending that Signature's system was not something that should have received a patent. In other words, the patent was granted for subject matter that did not fall into one of the patent categories: process, machine, manufacture, or composition of matter. The lower court ruled for State Street but the Federal Circuit reversed.

The Federal Circuit was not persuaded that "process" should be narrowly read. Unlike the Supreme Court, the Federal Circuit found significance in Congress' substitution of "process" for "art" in 1952. And "process" included business processes. Therefore, contrary to the lower court's holding, there was no business process exception to what was patentable. The Federal Circuit went even further, downplaying the four categories of patentable subject matter set forth in the Patent Act. Patentability "should not focus on which of the four categories of subject matter a claim is directed to—process, machine, manufacture, or composition of matter—but rather on the essential characteristics of the subject matter, in particular, its practical utility." (A claim in a patent is the legal description of the invention.) Expanding, the Federal Circuit seemed to declare that the test of patentability was whether the thing sought to be patented brought about a "useful, concrete, and tangible result." So much for statutory language.

State Street produced a run to the Patent Office. Small players in various corners of the business world saw not just the opportunity to enshrine their own ideas with patents but also the possibility of big bucks from licensing to others. Big players sought patents in part to protect themselves from such shakedowns. State Street particularly shook Wall Street. After all, the decision was about financial products and services. If these services required the assurance and protection of patent law, better get hopping.

Spurred by an increase in patent applications that seemed to involve ways of doing business, financial and otherwise, the Patent Office had already begun focusing on what some were calling business methods. The Patent Office has long had an elaborate, detailed system for classifying patent applications. In 1997, business, costing, and pricing sections of two existing classes were brought together in a new class, 705.[13] The new class included patent applications that some observers might not consider to be business methods, and other classes continued to include what some might call business methods, but the new 705 class was a rough approximation of activity regarding business methods patents. In 2000, a White Paper on Business Methods patents was issued.[14] The number of 705 class applications quickly grew, but growth in the number of patents granted was considerably slower (Table 2).

Table 2. Class 705 Applications and Patents

Fiscal Year	Class 705 Applications	Class 705 Patents
2009	8,229	1,725
2008	10,293	1,643
2007	9,843	1,333
2006	8,352	1,195
2005	6,976	711
2004	6,664	291
2003	6,383	486
2002	6,775	494
Source: USPTO Website, January 6, 2011.		

Several reasons probably accounted for the slow growth in granted patents. A general one was that the Information Age was causing an increase in many types of patent applications, and the Patent Office was falling behind in a number of patent classes. A more immediate reason was that business methods applications, particularly in fields such as finance, were a new, unfamiliar animal for the engineers and scientists who were the Patent Office's Examiners. Efforts to increase both the number of Examiners and their knowledge of fields beyond the traditional bailiwicks of patents took time.

For a while, rejection rates for patent applications in the 705 class were higher than for many other classes. Part of the reason was probably unfamiliarity, and part might have been negative reactions to some of the simplistic applications for what most observers would call everyday activities. The number of granted patents increased under the Department of Commerce and Patent Office leadership that assumed power following the elections of 2008. For business methods patents, not everyone would agree that the increase was a good thing.

Supreme Court Meets Information Age, Punts

The *State Street* patentability standard—useful, concrete, and tangible result—suffered a setback in October 2008, and at the hands of the very same court, the Federal Circuit, that had embraced the standard so enthusiastically ten years before. The case was *In Re Bilski*.[15] The issue was whether a method describing how to hedge the risk of price changes in commodities trading was patentable. The Federal Circuit said no. Lack of a useful, concrete, and tangible result was not the basis for the decision, however. That standard could provide useful indications of patentability, but it was insufficient for a firm determination. The test that the Federal Circuit now found appealing was machine-or-transformation: A process was "surely patent-eligible under §101 if: (1) it is tied to a particular machine or apparatus, or (2) it transforms a particular article into a different state or thing."[16] The hedging method did not meet the machine-or-transformation test. The Federal Circuit, however, did affirm its *State Street* holding that business methods were most assuredly patentable.

Bilski quickly made its way to the Supreme Court, and in late June of 2010 that body handed down a much anticipated decision. For those who desired clarification about the status of business methods patents, including software patents, the decision was disappointing.

In *Bilski v. Kappos*,[17] all nine of the Supreme Court Justices agreed that no patent should be granted for the described hedging process. The point all nine justices apparently agreed upon was that the process was abstract and therefore not patentable. But there was no single rationale that could provide much-needed guidance to the Patent Office and the patent and business communities. Four Justices—Kennedy, who wrote the opinion of the Court, Roberts, Thomas, and Alito—said as little as possible. They defined the proposed patent as an abstract concept and rejected it for abstractness. But they did not hold that business methods were unpatentable. Although business methods present special Information Age challenges—the opinion specifically recognized the existence of the Information Age—the four Justices found no general prohibition on the granting of patents for business methods.

Four other Justices—Stevens, who wrote a concurring opinion in the judgment, Breyer, who joined in that opinion and also wrote another concurring opinion in the judgment, Ginsburg, and Sotomayor would have prohibited business methods patents.

Justice Scalia joined portions of Kennedy's opinion and a portion of Breyer's opinion. The portions of Kennedy's opinion that Scalia did not join included the uneasy acceptance of patents on business methods; Scalia's acceptance of business methods patents seemed to be enthusiastic rather than uneasy. The portion of Breyer's opinion that Scalia did not join was the portion stating that patents on business methods should not be permitted, more evidence that Scalia was a supporter of patents on business methods.

Interestingly, the portions of Kennedy's opinion that Scalia did not join included the only portions of the opinion that referred to the Information Age. Being a firm Constitutional Originalist, maybe Justice Scalia objects to the Information Age.

Okay, perhaps a cheap shot at Justice Scalia. But he did seem to go out of his way to avoid acknowledging the facts of the Information Age and the difficulties they can create for statutory and Constitutional interpretation.

Thus *Bilski v. Kappos* left the issue of what was patentable in a very muddled state. The Supreme Court acknowledged as much by almost pleading with the Federal Circuit to produce a better standard for the patentability of so-called business methods patents. Four justices—Kennedy, Roberts, Thomas, and Alito—did specifically acknowledge the challenges of the Information Age for the patent system. For example,

> The Information Age empowers people with new capacities to perform statistical analyses and mathematical calculations with a speed and sophistication that enable the design of protocols for more efficient performance of a vast number of business tasks. If a high enough bar is not set when considering patent applications of this sort, patent examiners and courts could be flooded with claims that would put a chill on creative endeavor and dynamic change.[18]

Similarly, when discussing the machine-or-transformation test, which the Court held was a useful and important clue but not the sole test for the patentability of processes under §101 of the Patent Act:

> The machine-or-transformation test may well provide a sufficient basis for evaluating processes similar to those in the Industrial Age—for example, inventions grounded in a physical or other tangible form. But there are reasons to doubt whether the test should be the sole criterion for determining the patentability of inventions in the Information Age....[T]he machine-or-transformation test would create uncertainty as to the patentability of software, advanced diagnostic medicine techniques, and

> inventions based on linear programming, data compression, and the manipulation of digital signals. . . . Section 101's terms suggest that new technologies may call for new inquiries.[19]

Not that all of this theorizing seems to mean a great deal to the Patent Office. After years of criticism about few granted patents and slow application reviews, the Office, probably in part reflecting the priorities of the new leadership following the 2008 election, increased the output of 705 class patents in early 2010 and not only did not blink when the Supreme Court handed down *Bilski v. Kappos* in late June but actually upped production. The average weekly number of patents issued in the 705 class was 71 for the first six months of 2010. Following the Bilski decision, the weekly average for the last six months of the year was 85. And as for the standard the Office was following at the end of 2010, it almost appears that anything goes. For example, in November 2010, five months after the Supreme Court's decision, patents were granted in the 705 class for basing premium rates for travel accident insurance on the probability of an earthquake occurrence, for determining the covariance between different types of loans, and for developing retirement plans.[20]

Patenting Financial Complexity

As noted in the early part of this chapter, patents were not a cause, at least not a significant cause, of the financial meltdown that began in 2007-08. But patents do provide evidence of how complex the financial world has become, and complexity was a cause of the financial meltdown. Complexity helped unleash and expand the money creation process. Moreover, it was a volatile form of money that was created, money that could—and did—disappear as quickly as it appeared. The evidence provided by patents about financial complexity can be found in both patent assignees and patent subject matter.

Regarding assignees, patent applications are not filed by corporations or entities. They are filed by individuals. But frequently those individuals are employees of corporations or entities, or closely connected to them, and the patents are assigned to the sponsoring organization, hence the importance of assignees. In short, assignees are the heavy players in the patent arena.

The identity of some significant financial industry assignees for 705 class patents granted in the years 2007-2010 is given in Table 3, Financial Complexity Contributors. These patents were for applications filed in earlier years—sometimes four or more years earlier—and thus are evidence of ongoing practices for a considerable period prior to the actual granting of the patents. In other words, these patents, although granted after the commencement of the financial meltdown, are indicative of financial practices in the years that led to the meltdown.

Some readers might dispute the title of the table, Financial Complexity Contributors. After all, the patents all involve computer activities, and don't computer activities make things easier and more efficient for us humans? Well, perhaps at the individual activity level. But in combination, individual computer activities can lead to greater overall complexity, which thus far in the Information Age has produced some decidedly unpleasant situations, such as the financial meltdown that commenced in 2007-08. So the theoretical beneficial contribution to human welfare of a single patent for financial activities might turn negative when considered with other singularly beneficial contributions.

Turning from patent assignees to patent subject matter, very little of the financial world has escaped the efforts of financial engineers over the last decade or so to patent what they preach. Financial patents evidencing the growth in complexity that has contributed to a volatile money creation process can be categorized in a variety of ways. One way would be to focus on the tools of the patents, for example, modeling, simulation, and various mathematical procedures. This, however, can very quickly lead into an algorithmic swamp where such terminology as "multivariate distribution of barriers with exponential marginals" discourages all but the hardiest analyst (and incidentally puts many of the patents way over the heads of CEOs and other high level managers).[21]

Table 3. Financial Complexity Contributors (2007-2010)	
Bank of America	19
Barclays	10
Capital One	9
Citicorp	13
Credit Suisse First Boston	1
Exchanges[1]	64
Federal Reserve Banks	2
Freddie Mac, Fannie Mae	43
GE Financial	4
Goldman Sachs	43
JP Morgan Chase	94
Lehman Brothers	4
Morgan Stanley	57
PNC Financial Services	5
UBS	5
Vanguard	4
Wells Fargo	5

This table is a rough count of business methods patents granted to selected members of the financial industry. The count is limited to patents in the 705 class. Moreover, the count for an organization might not include all of its 705 class patents. Some 705 class patents resemble traditional machine, apparatus, and process patents and were thus excluded from the count of more ill-defined business methods patents. The analysis from which the count was derived was http://www.patentsbyfrip.com.

[1] Among others, includes Chicago Board Options Exchange, Chicago Mercantile Exchange, NASDAQ OMX Group, New York Stock Exchange, and various electronic exchanges.

Another approach focuses on purpose. Common, often overlapping, purposes of financial patents include: valuation of financial assets; creation of new financial assets; forecasting; development of financial strategies; and high speed trading. A brief description and an example are given in the following paragraphs for each of these five categories. Be prepared for a rough ride.

Valuation patents include those that purport to present a method for valuing financial assets. In September 2010, JP Morgan Chase Bank was granted a patent on a method of valuing assets, including interest-rate sensitive derivative securities.[22] The patent's full title was "Stabilized Monte Carlo Technique and Method and System of Applying Same to Valuate Assets Including Derivative Securities." The application had been filed in 2003. The valuation method called for: (1) the selection of a model equation; (2) the receipt of equation parameters such as current data, historical data, security-specific data, or general market data; (3) the generation of Monte Carlo paths; (4) the construction of a lattice of state variables; (5) the calculation of derived variables on the lattice; (6) the calculation of derived variables for each Monte Carlo path based on the derived variables on the lattice; (7) and finally the valuation of the security. And oh, with the caveat that the Monte Carlo path state variables were not restricted to the lattice node values.

New financial assets apparently find their way into the patent system as processes. They certainly aren't machines, manufactures, or compositions of matter. In 2002, the Federal National Mortgage Association—it prefers to be called Fannie Mae, perhaps to obfuscate its government connection—filed a patent application for a method of creating financial assets. The financial assets accentuate different types of sub-loan level risk associated with certain home mortgage loans and are configured to operate as hedges against risks that oppose the different types of sub-loan level risk. Yes, that's pretty much the wording from the patent. The financial assets are sold to different investors in the capital markets. The patent was granted in September 2010.[23] Given Fannie Mae's contribution to the financial downturn, one is tempted to conclude that this particular financial asset was less than a rousing success.

Forecasting is as integral to finance as it is to weather. In the simplest cases of financial forecasting, the future is just an extrapolation of a past trend. The simplest cases, however, quickly give way to the musings of financial engineers. In 2000, a major Wall Street investment bank, Lehman Brothers, applied for a patent on forecasting. The patent was granted in August 2007. Its title was "Methods and Systems for Analyzing and Predicting Market Winners and Losers."[24] The method began with the grouping of stocks into deciles based on net price performance over the preceding year. The top decile performers were referred to as "winners," and the bottom decile performers were referred to as "losers." A volume/turnover filter was applied to the groupings. The result was supposed to aid investors in predicting when to hold some stocks long and others short over various time periods, thereby maximizing the profitability of a portfolio. In September 2008, a little over a year after receiving the patent on predicting market winners and losers, Lehman Brothers filed for bankruptcy, an event that signaled the true magnitude of the troubles facing the world's financial and economic systems.

Financial strategies can be simple, and they can be complex. Financial engineers and the Patent Office seem to prefer complex. In June of 2010, Goldman Sachs was granted a patent entitled "System and Method for Algorithmic Trading Strategies."[25] The application had been originally filed in 2004. The system and method involved executing an order to trade a security. First, a value x representing a percentage of market volume associated with the security was to be obtained. Then expected market impacts, expected price risks, and expected total costs of executing the trade over multiple time periods was to be calculated. Finally, the order was to be executed "by at least a first component and a second component in tandem over a time period at which the calculated expected total cost is minimized for the value x, wherein the first component adjusts trade parameters to maximize spread capture, and the second component determines pockets of liquidity at optimal price points."[26] With such a strategy, how can a trader lose?

High speed, largely automated, trading—also called electronic trading—in the securities and derivatives markets exploded in the first decade of the 21st Century. Consequences of this development are touched upon in the next chapter. For the purposes of this chapter's focus on patents, it is sufficient to note that the race to patent trading technology is turning into a stampede. Many patent applications are from firms specializing in technology and not well known to the general public. But big names on Wall Street can be found. In March 2010, Morgan Stanley received a patent entitled "Low Latency Trading System."[27] The application had been filed in 2007. Latency is the time interval between when a trading engine sends a trade order to an exchange and when the trade order is acknowledged and acted upon by the exchange. A low latency trading environment is one in which a few milliseconds can be the difference between a winning trade and a losing trade.

* * *

To reiterate the point made at the beginning of this chapter on patents. The financial meltdown that commenced in 2007-08 was not caused by patents. But patents provide evidence of the underlying cause: the increasing financialization of the nation's economy that in turn is a consequence of the Information Age and its tool, the computer. And the patent system's own muddled response to Information Age developments is an example of how paradigms across societies and cultures are being shaken.

6

Financialism

As described in the preceding chapters, one consequence of the computer-based Information Age is a financial sector that over the last three decades has grown more than any other broad sector of the U.S. economy. To say it a bit more concisely, the U.S. financial sector has gotten proportionally larger. Has this growth peaked? Is the financial sector's current elevated position the new norm? What portion of the growth in financial assets is the result of real economic growth, and what portion is wishful thinking? Will the ongoing financial difficulties lead to a permanent financial sector retrenchment? Does a larger financial sector mean greater wealth for all? For some?

Only the passage of time will provide meaningful data regarding such questions. But absent a worldwide conflagration or a successful Luddite-like effort to exterminate computers (maybe not a bad idea), it seems safe to conclude that information has become a cheap commodity. And as has been argued in earlier chapters, money is just a form of information. It is information about supply and demand, about how valuable something is to a seller and a purchaser.

So if money is just a form of information and if the Information Age is about the proliferation of information, might the Information Age also be about the proliferation of money? But if that is the case, why aren't we all rich? An answer from standard economic theory might be inflation: all other things being equal, an increase in the supply of money leads to increases in nominal prices, or inflation. But does this explanation from standard theory really fit the Information Age's relationship between money and information?

A more speculative explanation might be that in the Information Age, wealth tends to accrue to those with both access to and the ability to use information. Since access to information in the Information Age is relatively unrestrained, the key is the ability to make use of the information. Those who have the ability, become wealthy. What about those who don't? This may be where the promise of the Information Age runs into difficulties. Those unskilled in the use of the fundamental commodity of the Information Age—information—might be a drag on overall wealth. Not only are the unskilled unable—there are exceptions, of course—to use information to create wealth, they also face declining markets for what they can do. Service industries, a major employer of the unskilled, are becoming increasingly automated. Witness the help desk. Your call is screened, endlessly it often seems, before you finally get a human being. And more and more often, your problem is allegedly solved before the arrival of an actual human voice.

Thus, some economic players in the Information Age become wealthier. But others become less wealthy, at least proportionally. Eventually, wealth distribution in some form—jobless benefits, universal health care—might be necessary. Pressures will rise to share the wealth created by the ability to use information with those who are casualties of the Information Age.

Having raised but not resolved a number of issues about the new economic environment of the Information Age, let's consider another one. What does the Information Age and the rise of finance mean for the leading current generalizations about national economies: capitalism and socialism?

Time for a New Ism?

Remember feudalism? How about mercantilism? For those who did not sleep through history classes, perhaps the terms ring a bell. They are terms that attempt to categorize forms of societal, political, and economic organization in times gone by. Feudalism is applied most often to Medieval Europe, medieval meaning from sometime in the latter part of the First Millennium through approximately the 15th Century. Feudal societies were hierarchical and organized around land. Lords granted fiefs, or parcels of land, to vassals in return for services performed by the vassals. Often the services were of a military nature. A king was the most powerful lord of a geographic area, which today would be called a country or nation. At the bottom of the arrangement were peasants. A central theme in the history of Medieval Europe is the evolution of the rights and responsibilities among lords and vassals, with control of land—for primarily agricultural purposes—being a central focus.

Mercantilism followed feudalism, not necessarily replacing it but reflecting the growth of commercial activity, particularly international trade. One definition is "economic nationalism for the purpose of building a wealthy and powerful state."[1] The overriding goal was to achieve and maintain a favorable balance of trade—for exports to exceed imports, for gold and silver inventories to grow. That goal was pretty much the dominant one in Western European countries from the 15th to the 18th Centuries. Even today, many nations display a mercantilistic attitude in that a favorable balance of trade is considered desirable.

The preceding brief summaries of feudalism and mercantilism should be approached warily. Unlike today, only a small portion of premodern populations conversed about economic abstracts. Indeed, the term feudalism does not appear to have been in use during feudal times. It originated in the efforts of later historians to describe how society and economics functioned in the Middle Ages.

Accompanying the beginnings of the Industrial Age in the late 18th Century was a blossoming of economic thought and theory, much of it intertwined with political thought and theory. Adam Smith's seminal work, *The Wealth of Nations*, was published in 1776. Smith saw three factors of production: land, labor, and capital. He likened the operation of markets to an "invisible hand." The result of each individual pursuing his or her own needs and wants was an overall benefit for society as a whole, although "hers" were rarely recognized as independent actors in those days. Among other notables in these formative years of modern economic thought and theory were: Thomas Malthus (1766-1834), who wrote on population growth and its consequences; David Ricardo (1772-1823), who developed a theory of comparative advantage under which nations and individuals specialize in the economic activities each does best; and John Stuart Mill (1806-1873), who espoused individual liberty and utilitarianism, the latter holding that an individual should act so as to produce the greatest happiness for the greatest number of people.

Comparative advantage, utilitarianism, the invisible hand, individual liberty—yes, the point where economic thought and theory left off and political thought and theory began was often unclear. And remains so to this day.

Knowledge of the thoughts and theories of Smith, Malthus, Ricardo, Mill, their notable contemporaries, and the big thinkers who followed them—Karl Marx, Alfred Marshall, John Maynard Keynes, Friedrich Hayek, Milton Friedman, Ayn Rand (hey, she had impact), to name a few—was not confined to society's elites. Other blossomings brought about by the Industrial Age were education and publishing for the masses, or at least sizeable portions of those masses.

Opinions about economic and political abstracts became more and more widespread, as did the accompanying debates and controversies. The result is a world in which homage is not only paid to a nation-state, or perhaps a religion, or both, but also very likely to an economic-political abstract. Today, the two dominant such abstracts are capitalism and socialism. How those two rose to the fore is really a history of the last 250 years, a panoramic history beyond the scope of this work. The focus herein is the present, and at present, capitalism and socialism dominate the game. Communism, which might be considered an extreme form of socialism, was until several decades ago a major contender and is still lurking on the sidelines. But for the moment, at least in most industrial economies, capitalism and socialism are the principal economic-political isms vying for men's (and women's) souls.

Neither, however, has a precise definition. Indeed, if the variants of each are considered, the picture quickly becomes Picassoesque. Very generally, capitalism describes an economic system, buttressed by appropriate political philosophies, in which market forces and private ownership of the means of production are the rule. And also very generally, socialism describes an economic system, similarly buttressed by appropriate political philosophies, in which ownership and administration of the means of production reside to a considerable extent with government or worker organizations, and government has an extensive say in the allocation of resources.

In the rhetoric arena, the many complexities and nuances of capitalism and socialism, and the fact that a pure form of neither is to be found in the real world, are often lost. From the capitalism camp, the perceived opponent—full-fledged enemy to some—is reduced to "government control." Anything that smacks of government control is socialism and, therefore, harmful to capitalism.

Many practical-minded people see the current economic arrangements in most economically advanced nations, particularly the United States, as a mixture, a mixture that varies from nation to nation but still a mixture. Generalizing about the United States, the private sector is the dominant economic driver, private ownership of businesses is the norm, but the public, government presence is far from insignificant. Government not only maintains rules—antitrust, for example—aimed at ensuring a degree of fair economic play in the private sector but also controls the sources of some raw materials, influences the allocation of resources, mandates redistributions of wealth—the progressive income tax, social security, health care—and actually oversees some businesses, particularly in times of economic troubles.

This mixture of private and public economic components is actually referred to in some textbooks and other materials as a mixed economy. For example, in the 1976 edition of his classic textbook *Economics*, Paul Samuelson wrote: "Capitalism in the sense of undiluted laissez-faire, died before Queen Victoria died. And most of this book has been concerned with describing the mixed economy which buried it."[2]

Today's problem with the capitalism versus socialism debate is its Industrial Age context. The Information Age is well underway yet capitalism and socialism are attacked and defended—capitalism particularly—with little attention paid to the vast technological, economic, and cultural transformations underway. The ultimate cause of these transformations is the tsunami of information. Where does information fall in Adam Smith's three factors of production: land, labor, and capital? Traditionalists might argue that it is a form of capital, and to an extent they would be correct. But the quantity, pervasiveness, and importance of information raise this form of capital to a level of dominance unimaginable during much of the Industrial Age. To quote an article from a preeminent admirer of capitalism, *The Economist*, "Data are becoming the new raw material of business: an economic input almost on a par with capital and labor."[3] And maybe the "almost" should be removed.

As was described in previous chapters, the Information Age has moved financial assets and the financial industry from enablers of economic activity to major components of economic activity, indeed in some cases seemingly the sole object of economic activity. A way of looking at the current condition is that two economies now exist where formerly there was only one. That one was the economy that produced things from Adam Smith's land, labor, and capital. That economy had a quantifiable annual production. That economy worked well enough to produce a surplus, which was wealth. But then the computer brought about another economy, an economy that took information as its major input, combined the information with existing wealth, and produced still more wealth. Only this additional wealth has a decidedly chimerical aspect.[4]

Another way to view the impact of the computer and the Information Age is in terms of capacity. The vast amount of information now available just might have created a semi-permanent state of financial excess capacity. One analysis—admittedly not widely accepted—of the savings and loan and banking crises of the 1980s and very early 1990s argued that they were in large measure the result of excess capacity.[5] The excess capacity was in turn a product of laws restricting banks and savings and loans to operations in only one state and to basic banking products and services. These laws had been in existence for much of the nation's history. Initially, they were compatible with the environment dictated by the marketplace. As time passed, however, technology gradually altered that environment. The natural markets for banking products and services were no longer confined to a few products and services in a limited geographic area. The developing Information Age accelerated the marketplace changes. But the now outdated laws prevented the banking industry from evolving and consolidating. Two results of the anachronistic legal structure were more banks and savings and loans than the marketplace could support over the long term, and a large number of small monopolies; in other words, excess capacity.

Computer technology did enable banks, savings and loans, and other financial players—money market mutual funds, for example—to ameliorate somewhat on the product side the effects of the anachronistic legal structure. The geographic restrictions, however, remained a major impediment to needed industry consolidation. That excess capacity indeed existed can be deduced from the number of institutions that disappeared during the period. Between 1980 and 1995, the number of banks in the nation declined from 14,435 to 9,940, and the number of savings and loans and other thrifts from 4,005 to 1,437.[6] Some of the disappearances were due to outright failures. Others were due to mergers and acquisitions, often encouraged by the government.

The troubles that exploded on the financial industry in 2007-08 can also be viewed as an excess capacity problem. The industry has been given a tool—the computer—that can produce enormous amounts of apparent wealth with minimal human effort. Think about it. This is a form of excess capacity. In the earlier crises of the 1980s and early 1990s, the solution to excess capacity was two-pronged. First, the government—primarily through the Federal Deposit Insurance Corporation and the specially created Resolution Trust Corporation—aggressively confronted the problem of troubled institutions, ultimately reducing their number. Second, the causes of the excess capacity, those causes being the anachronistic legal barriers to product and geographic evolution, were removed. In the current crisis, government is again involved in overseeing the demise or restructuring of troubled institutions. But the "how" of controlling the excess capacity creator—the computer—is at the moment not readily apparent. More on this problem in the final chapter, and on one of those legal barriers, the Glass-Steagall Act, that some observers now want back.

A further thought on capitalism and the Information Age concerns the future, and appropriateness, of the growth model prevalent in modern economies. Underlying capitalism is the premise that society as a whole benefits most when each individual is free to pursue his or her own wants and needs—within reason, many would add. The individual's pursuit of his or her own course results in overall economic growth. But another way of describing capitalism is not quite as attractive: "capitalism is premised on scarcity and requires all of us to compete against each other relentlessly."[7] Is growth compatible with this concept of capitalism?

In any case, the growth model seems most valid when resources are readily available and negative by-products are at a minimum. A number of commentators, however, argue that these pre-conditions are starting to evaporate. Raw material resources are being depleted, and negative by-products—pollution, climate change, international transfers of wealth and debt—are increasing. Thomas Friedman has asked the basic questions:

> What if the crisis of 2008 represents something much more fundamental than a deep recession? What if it's telling us that the whole growth model we created over the last 50 years is simply unsustainable economically and ecologically and that 2008 was when we hit the wall—when Mother Nature and the market both said: "No more."[8]

Concerns are not limited to such critics of the status quo as Friedman. Even that staunch supporter of capitalism, *The Economist*, sometimes expresses wariness:

> *The Economist* puts more faith in business than most. Yet even the stolidest defenders of capitalism would, by and large, agree that its tendency to form cartels, shuffle off the costs of pollution and collapse under the weight of its own financial inventiveness needs to be constrained by laws designed to channel its energy to the general good.[9]

"[C]ollapse under the weight of its own financial inventiveness. . . ." Intriguing words, those.

Perhaps the time has arrived for a new ism. After all, feudalism, mercantilism, and numerous other models of human economic-political history have faded away. In spite of the contentions of some of their supporters, capitalism and socialism are not set in concrete. They are not anointed in the Bible or other religious tract. They are merely descriptions. And they are descriptions that imply a certain freedom of choice, freedom to select the extent to which collective action is allowed to control economic activity. Capitalism leans towards less collective action, socialism towards more. But the ability of a human group, such as a nation, to decide where on the capitalism-socialism spectrum it wishes to reside is assumed. The inundation of information brought by the computer, however, may be reducing the range of that choice. Increasingly, the choice may be merely a reaction to the spreading tentacles of the Information Age.

So what should a new economic-political paradigm be called? Infoism? Certainly not a very compelling word. How about financialism? It's got an ism, and the Information Age has certainly spawned an Age of Finance. In any event, capitalism and socialism are of the Industrial Age. The Information Age is well underway, rendering Industrial Age paradigms obsolete. Human thinking needs to catch up.

Interlude: Nuclear Doomsday

One of the more remembered movies of the 1960s is the Stanley Kubrick tour de force, *Dr. Strangelove*, with, among others, Peter Sellers (in three roles), George C. Scott, Sterling Hayden, and Slim Pickens. The movie ends with a montage of exploding nuclear weapons to the tune of the nostalgic, melancholy song "We'll Meet Again." The nukes are going off because, unbeknownst to the American government and military, the Soviets have constructed a Doomsday Machine that guarantees world nuclear annihilation if even one nuclear weapon explodes on a target in the Soviet Union. And oh, the Doomsday Machine can't be disarmed. The Russkies, as the Slim Pickens character, Major "King Kong," calls the Soviets, hadn't gotten around to telling the rest of the world of the Doomsday Machine's existence. It was to be a surprise announcement at an upcoming Communist Party Congress.

Through a series of unlikely events and circumstances—that in hindsight were not all that unlikely—the Americans set off the Doomsday Machine. Certain U.S. field commanders had been granted authority to conduct retaliatory nuclear strikes if Washington and the U.S. national leadership are wiped out. One of those field commanders, General Jack D. Ripper played by Sterling Hayden, is mentally unbalanced but not in a way that his peers and superiors, particularly those of a similar political persuasion, might recognize. General Ripper takes advantage of a training exercise and orders a nuclear attack on the Soviets. In spite of the efforts of both the Soviets and the Americans, one of Ripper's B-52s, piloted by Slim Picken's Major Kong, delivers a nuke. And Doomsday commences.

Among the messages of the movie: humans can develop technology that can byte back, whoops, bite back really, really bad.

The workings of the Doomsday Machine in *Dr. Strangelove* were not detailed, but even in those very early days of computers the writers likely had computer technology in mind. Computers were certainly at the heart of another doomsday-theme movie, 1983's *WarGames* starring Matthew Broderick and Ally Sheedy. A much lighter work, with a feel-good ending, *WarGames* had computers galore. Broderick's character David, a teenage computer-nerd whiz, uses his computer and modem to hack into his school's computer system. He changes a failing grade he had received, and grades of his friend Jennifer, who is Sheedy's character. In a search for computer games, he sets his computer loose on the local phone system. His computer stumbles onto a connection to a supercomputer, WOPR (pronounced "Whopper"), at the North American Aerospace Defense Command (NORAD) facility in Cheyenne Mountain, Colorado. WOPR is programmed to simulate war games. It also has been given a degree of autonomy over America's Intercontinental Ballistic Missiles (ICBMs) in their silos. Previously, a test had revealed that some of the human missile controllers in the silos were reluctant to actually fire the bad boys. So the unreliable humans were replaced by the dispassionate and supposedly dependable computer.

WOPR, however, is not completely understood by those who have given it such power. Not knowing that he has contacted a potential doomsday machine, David engages it in a game of Global Thermonuclear War. After a series of adventures, disaster in the form of an all-out nuclear exchange between the United States and the Soviet Union is barely averted when David causes WOPR to play itself in an unwinnable game of tic-tac-toe, which causes the supercomputer to crash. Presumably, humans retake control of the missile silos.

Dr. Strangelove and *WarGames* were fiction, but nuclear war close-calls attributable to technology have indeed occurred. One day in October 1960, the NORAD warning system indicated that the Soviets had launched a massive missile strike against the United States. The system's level of certainty was 99.9 percent. Turns out a radar facility in Thule, Greenland, had misinterpreted the rising moon.[10]

On June 3, 1980, a computerized display at the Strategic Air Command in Omaha, Nebraska, showed two inbound submarine-launched ballistic missiles. Eighteen seconds later, the number increased. After three plus minutes of heightened alert and incipient war moves, lack of supporting data led cooler heads to prevail. A similar false alarm occurred three days later. The cause of the incidents was eventually determined: the failure of a single integrated chip in a computer that was part of a communication system.[11]

And on September 26, 1983, a Soviet early warning satellite sent a signal that a nuclear missile had been launched, probably by the United States and probably at the Soviet Union. Signals indicating four more missiles quickly followed. The officer on duty in the command bunker, Stanislav Petrov, hesitated. If it really were a nuclear attack, many more missiles should have been evident. And ground-based radar was showing nothing. The alleged incoming missiles had already been reported to higher command and, at a time of very high tensions between the U.S. and the Soviet Union, might have led to a retaliation order. But Petrov made a determination that it was a false alarm, a determination that possibly kept the Cold War from becoming World War III. The false alarm was later traced to the satellite misinterpreting the sun reflecting off clouds; the satellite "thought" the reflected sun was a missile launch.[12]

Why Not a Financial Doomsday?

Nuclear war is by no means the only area in which computers in the Information Age have shown a capacity for mischief. Thanks to computers, finance has also experienced moments on the precipice.

In four trading days in October 1987—Wednesday the 14th through Monday the 19th—the Dow Jones Industrial Average fell 769 points, or 31 percent. This represented a loss of $1 trillion in the value of outstanding stocks. The Presidential Task Force, chaired by Secretary of the Treasury Nicholas F. Brady, that examined the market drop cited specific triggering events: an unexpectedly high merchandise trade deficit that pushed interest rates to new high levels, and proposed tax legislation that led to the collapse of the stocks of a number of takeover candidates.[13] More generally, the Task Force also alluded to "imbalances in the budget, foreign transactions, savings, corporate assets positions and other fundamental factors."

The initial declines "ignited mechanical, price-insensitive selling by a number of institutions employing portfolio insurance strategies" and mutual funds reacting to redemptions. As the selling escalated, aggressive trading organizations, anticipating a continuation of the trend, got into the game, further contributing to the drops in stock prices.

In its report, the Task Force acknowledged that markets were changing. The traditional view of separate markets for stocks, stock index futures, and stock options needed to give way to the reality that for some purposes the markets were in fact one. Technology had increased the interconnections, and the oversight structure should be adjusted accordingly. The separate agencies that regulated the different markets needed better coordination. This required not an abolishment of existing agencies but the giving of coordination authority for critical intermarket issues to a single agency. Those intermarket issues included clearing and credit mechanisms, margin requirements, circuit breaker mechanisms such as price limits and trading halts, and information systems for monitoring activities across markets.

What is intriguing about a hindsight look at the Task Force's report, however, is the apparent acceptance with little question of the "mechanical, price-insensitive selling by a number of institutions employing portfolio insurance strategies." Computers, not humans, were making trading decisions, and no one seemed to find that too troubling. No one appeared to have asked the question, where is this headed?

That unanswered question still hangs in the air.

On May 6, 2010, the Dow Jones Industrial Average fell nearly 1,000 points, most of it in a short period after 2 p.m. The event has been dubbed the Flash Crash. The market rebounded before the close of business for the day but was still down 348 points from the opening. During its momentary trough, a number of stocks were virtually valueless. No single cause has been identified, but high-speed, computerized trading was certainly part of the action. A preliminary joint report by the Securities and Exchange Commission and the Commodity Futures Trading Commission listed a number of initial actions being taken and a number of topics needing further study.[14]

But perhaps more interesting than the details was the implicit identification of three broader trends. One is simply speed. Trading is now measured in microseconds.[15] Indeed, news reports in 2009 and 2010 indicate that the time it takes to wink can mean big bucks. For example, a June 2010 article in *The Wall Street Journal* described how some investment firms were gaining a trading advantage by buying premium access to data feeds from exchanges.[16] This gave the firms a 100 to 200 milliseconds advantage over investors using standard market tools. Directing the data into supercomputers might result in savings of only pennies per share, but that becomes serious money when multiplied by thousands of trades. High speed trading comes in various forms that together were estimated in the article to account for approximately two-thirds of stock market volume.

A second trend evident from an examination of the SEC-CFTC report is the changing location of trading. In 2005, the New York Stock Exchange accounted for 79.1 percent of the trading in NYSE-listed stocks. Just four years later, in 2009, the NYSE share had fallen to 25.1 percent. The major trading venues were (1) register exchanges such as the NYSE, (2) electronic communications networks, (3) dark pools that offered trading services to institutional investors and others seeking to execute large trades, and (4) broker-dealers that executed trades internally. The latter two venues, which accounted for approximately 25 percent of trading in September 2009, did not display quotations in the composite quotation data widely distributed to the public.[17]

The third trend is the growth of high frequency trading, much of which is probably also high speed trading. High frequency trading is primarily the province of proprietary traders using computerized systems. They often submit very large orders based on complex strategies. In other words, they are the quintessential financial engineers. The SEC-CFTC report said that high frequency traders often account for 50 percent or more of daily trading volume.[18]

In both the 1988 Brady Commission Task Force report on the October 1987 market crash and the SEC-CFTC preliminary report on the May 2010 events, major recommendations involved circuit breakers. If various specified price movements hit certain triggers, trading is halted for specified times. Circuit breakers, price movement limits, and the like certainly seem useful. But there is a troubling aspect to such recommendations. They're like time-out in kindergarten: Johnny and Suzy get too exuberant, so quiet time in the corner. As computers get even more powerful, as the growth of trading volume continues outstripping traditional benchmarks, as power to move prices accrues more and more to a small group of high frequency traders, will an occasional quiet time be sufficient to regain control? Is no one in the financial industry or its regulatory structure contemplating the possibility of a complete collapse of financial markets? What is the chance that a future stoked-by-technology market meltdown will take the economy with it? Is the last bulwark against financial Armageddon really just a Johnny-and-Suzy time-out?

Other Notable Computer Glitches

The modern car has evolved into a very complicated computer system. Sensors, microprocessors, algorithms, as much as 100 million lines of computer code—this isn't the mechanical machine of thirty or forty years ago, something maintained with just wrenches, pliers, and screwdrivers. No, the modern car is the province of computer and electrical engineers. And just as the case with other computer systems that have become fundamental to life in the 21st Century, things can go wrong, unexpected things difficult to isolate and identify.

In the fall of 2009, the media devoted considerable attention to unintended acceleration problems in certain Toyota vehicles. Simple physical phenomena—sticky pedals and interfering floor mats—were one explanation for the difficulties drivers were reporting. But other explanations were also advanced. One study had found that the portion of complaints to federal regulators about Toyotas and "speed control" tripled after electronic throttles were introduced in 2002.[19] Electronic throttles are a form of computer system. At one point, the owner's manual of Toyota's Camry cautioned about two-way radio systems affecting the electronic throttle system. In February 2011, the National Highway Traffic Safety Administration and the National Aeronautics and Space Administration released the findings of a ten-month study that found no evidence of an electronic cause of unintended acceleration in Toyotas. Not all critics were convinced, however.[20] The National Academy of Sciences is also studying the matter. Its report is expected later in the year.

In June 2009, a computer system was at fault in a Metrorail crash in Washington, D.C., killing nine. The National Transportation Safety Board concluded that the automatic train control system stopped detecting the presence of a train, causing the train to stop but also allowing speed commands to be transmitted to an approaching train.[21] The Washington accident is one of a number of incidents involving automated systems in trains, ships, and especially planes.[22] On one hand, these automated systems appear to have improved the safety of travel. On the other hand, accidents still occur, and the difficulties of integrating a largely passive human monitor into a system as a final fail safe seem to have increased. As the automation becomes more pervasive, keeping the human monitors focused becomes more problematic. An example is an October 2009 incident involving a Northwest Airlines Flight that was on automatic pilot and overshot Minneapolis-St. Paul by 150 miles as the human pilots were apparently engaged in an animated discussion on crew scheduling.

Open the Pod Bay Doors, Hal

But looking at individual accidents, even nuclear ones, is treating the computer as just another piece of technology, largely benign but with a problem from time to time. The computer is more than just another piece of technology producing incremental changes in how humans work, communicate, and travel. As described in the discussion of capitalism and other isms earlier in this chapter, the computer has introduced a new era, the Information Age, in which fundamental aspects of the human experience are being called into question.

Take war. Except for religion, perhaps nothing has had a more conspicuous presence in human history than war. The tools of warfare have certainly changed over the millennia, particularly over the most recent centuries. Horses, catapults, the long bow, gunpowder, rapid fire weapons, the submarine, the airplane—each added a new degree of lethality to war. But a basic element of war—human decision-making—remained constant. Only in fiction, *Dr. Strangelove* and *WarGames*, for example, was human control almost completely removed.

Within just the last few years, however, warfare has entered the robotic era.[23] Since 2003, when U.S. forces advanced sans robots from Kuwait to Baghdad, 7,000 unmanned aircraft and 12,000 robotic ground vehicles have become part of the U.S. arsenal. These tools have a variety of tasks, such as locating explosives, seeking out snipers, and bombing al-Qaeda hideouts. Human operation of these tools is still the norm, but in some cases the operators are half-a-world away, at bases in the United States. And in some cases, the only decision by the human operator is a veto. For example, the Counter-Rocket Artillery and Mortar (C-RAM) can react with sufficient speed to detect and destroy incoming rockets and missiles. A human operator can override a decision by the machine to fire, but the human has less than a second to exercise that control.

So the future of warfare might be battling robots over which humans have only precarious control. What will be the impact on the laws of war, on conflict resolution, on diplomacy, on international relations, on the apparent human need for dangerous challenges and heroism?

Despite its ubiquitous presence in history, warfare is not something that most humans experience directly. But just about everyone experiences work. What is the future of work in the Information Age?

If you're a computer, you're in great shape. Or at least your species is in great shape. Your kind is everywhere and is taking on more and more tasks. If you're a human, however, things might not be as rosy. In the past, technology has certainly changed the nature of work without significantly altering the overall need for workers. Mechanization reduced the number of farm workers needed, but the growth of factories took up the slack. Productivity increases attributable in large measure to technology and the movement of jobs to lower wage areas of the world reduced the number of factory workers needed, but the growth of service industries such as health care provided alternatives.

But as *Wall Street Journal* columnist David Wessel argues, "nothing in the textbooks says that the supply and demand for workers will intersect at a wage that is socially acceptable."[24] The high end—skilled workers, including those really proficient in computer stuff—is probably in good shape, as is the low end, service workers. But will there be enough jobs in the middle? Wessel describes the middle as jobs not requiring much education, jobs such as plumbers, electricians, and software technicians. But these jobs might actually be growth candidates. Another part of the middle consists of office workers, bureaucrats, paper shufflers. This part of the middle could be the most threatened by the Information Age. The automation of information creation, storage, and dissemination could be the death knell of, to use a 1950s categorization, many an Organization Man.

One option to care for the displaced Organization Men and other possible victims of the Information Age is biblical: have the rich subsidize the poor. When one considers the extravagant compensation some financial engineers and their Wall Street peers have received in recent years, a little sharing of the wealth, while obviously not very capitalistic, doesn't seem all that bad. A bit of ideological compromise would probably be agreeable to all but the true believers.

But what if the future of work is considerably more shaky? What if it is the Singularity, a utopia to some, a decidedly less attractive concept to others?

In the context of technology, the Singularity refers roughly to a merging of man and machine. As popularized by Raymond Kurzweil in his books *The Age of Intelligent Machines* (1990), *The Age of Spiritual Machines* (1999), and *The Singularity Is Near: When Humans Transcend Biology* (2005), the Singularity possibly arrives around 2045 and is the point when artificial intelligence (AI) surpasses human intelligence.[25] Machines are in charge, but it's not as if they are readily distinguishable from humans. Advances (or something) in biology, nanotechnology, and robotics have evolved at least some humans to a post-human, cyborgic state.

Sounds fanciful to some, but to others the study of rapid technological change and its challenges for human institutions, culture, and indeed existence is serious stuff. In 2008, Singularity University (SU) came into existence. Its corporate founders were Google, ePlanet Ventures, Autodesk, and Thusfar. Leasing facilities at the NASA Ames campus in Silicon Valley, California, SU offers an annual ten-week Graduate Studies Program and shorter executive programs during the year. The stated mission of SU is "to assemble, educate, and inspire leaders who understand and develop exponentially advancing technologies to address humanity's Grand Challenges."[26]

What should lesser mortals conclude from such concepts as the Singularity, from such efforts at understanding as SU, and from such occurrences as the triumph of the IBM supercomputer Watson on Jeopardy? Perhaps just that change is accelerating faster than ever before in human history, and where the Information Age is quickly leading might be far removed from such concepts as capitalism, socialism, and the like. Or more disturbingly, perhaps what's ahead is a planet on which humans have inadvertently ceded far too much control to computers and are reduced to pleading, "Open the pod bay doors, Hal."[27]

But let's leave the heavy thinking to those attending Singularity U and get back to the here and now.

7

Financial Oversight for the Information Age

The financial sector of the economy—banks, securities firms, insurance providers, and the many varieties and offshoots of each—has long been of special interest to government. One reason is simply that the financial sector is where the money is, or at least passes through. Of equal importance is that troubles in the financial sector can have significant impacts throughout the economy.

Government oversight of the financial sector is a perpetual work in progress. The inexorable march of technology both lessens over time the effectiveness of existing legal frameworks for supervising the sector and presents new, and thus initially unsupervised, areas for profit-making activities, or some would say, mischief. The law of unintended consequences enthusiastically does its thing: responses to one problem or crisis often lay the groundwork for a future problem or crisis. The popularities of various political and economic paradigms wax and wane. Only utopians can truly believe in the possibility of achieving, whether through an oversight system on one hand or the unfettered dominance of the marketplace on the other, a perfect financial sector. And in any event, agreement on what constitutes perfection itself is most likely beyond reach.

A Brief History

In the United States, the national government was not for several decades after its establishment much involved in the oversight of private sector finance. Indeed, although lacking explicit authorization in the Constitution, the national government was initially in the banking business as a participant. Among the powers granted to Congress in

Section 8, Article I, of the Constitution were the powers to borrow money, to regulate interstate and foreign commerce, to coin money and regulate its value, and to establish uniform bankruptcy laws—nothing about either overseeing finance or participating in financial activities other than as a borrower. At the time of the Constitution's preparation, only three banks existed in the fledging nation.[1]

But the national government shortly had its own bank. In February 1791, President George Washington signed an act, passed by Congress, incorporating the Bank of the United States (later called the First Bank of the United States). The Bank was authorized to issue capital subscriptions of $10 million, of which $2 million was to be held by the government. The chief proponent of the Bank was Secretary of the Treasury Alexander Hamilton. He saw the institution as a way of dealing with war debt, facilitating government finances, and most controversially, contributing to the nation's economic development by making commercial loans.[2]

The Bank's charter expired in 1811. But the financial turmoil in the aftermath of the War of 1812 and the activities of the many banks that had been chartered by states since the early 1790s soon persuaded Congress that a successor was needed. Thus the Second Bank of the United States was chartered in 1816. It was the first effort by the national government to bring a degree of oversight to the developing banking system. The Second Bank was charged primarily with promoting a uniform currency by getting banks to resume specie payments. It also functioned as a clearinghouse, holding large quantities of other banks' notes in reserve and threatening to redeem notes of banks that it considered to be over-issuing notes. "In this way, it functioned as an early bank regulator, a crucial function of the modern Fed."[3]

Students of U.S. history have some familiarity with the prominence and contentiousness of the First and Second Banks of the United States. Leading the opposition to the creation of the First Bank in 1790-91 were Thomas Jefferson and James Madison. The broad matters at issue—strict versus relaxed interpretation of the Constitution, the role of the national government in economic activity, the status quo versus change, agrarians versus business—were decided against Jefferson and

Madison and for Hamilton in this first instance. But the issues remained, festered, and are still very much a central part of the national dialogue. The agrarians-versus-business element has morphed into something a bit different, maybe small business versus big business, but the underlying class-conflict nature still exists.

Jefferson and Madison may have lost the argument about the First Bank, but their ideological successor, Andrew Jackson, triumphed over the Second Bank. He refused to renew the Second Bank's charter and withdrew federal deposits from it. Its charter expired in 1836, and it went bankrupt a few years later.

The Civil War helped return the national government to the financial oversight business. To facilitate the financing of the war, the United States established a national banking system under a new agency, the Office of the Comptroller of the Currency (OCC). A national charter could be obtained for a bank. Unlike state banks, the national banks could not issue their own notes. Instead, national banks issued government-printed notes, and to do so they had to purchase federal bonds. The national banking system did not, as some proponents hoped, drive state banks out of existence, but a tax on state bank notes did end that form of money. For the first time, the nation had a uniform currency.

Over the next four decades of the Industrial Age, the dual banking system in the United States—national banks and state banks—provided fuel and lubricant for economic growth. But the process was not painless, and the financial system was far from a model of stability. Financial panics in 1873, 1893, and 1907 resulted in bank failures and recessions. National and state banks were individually subject to varying degrees of oversight, but the financial system as a whole was largely unwatched and unsupervised by government. The panic in 1907 and subsequent recession persuaded many policymakers and members of the financial industry that a centralized authority was needed. The result was the passage of the Federal Reserve Act of 1913 and the creation of the Federal Reserve System, which was only partially centralized as considerable power was given to twelve Federal Reserve District Banks.

What was the purpose of this partly centralized authority? As set forth in the Federal Reserve Act, the purpose was "to furnish an elastic currency, to afford means of rediscounting commercial paper, to establish a more effective supervision of banking in the United States, and for other purposes."[4] Over time, the elastic currency purpose, in the form of monetary policy, came to dominate. The Fed does exercise or share supervisory authority over a substantial segment of the commercial banking industry, but monetary policy is what it is known for. Moreover, its interest in and enthusiasm for supervision have at times been decidedly lacking, as during the Greenspan era, 1987 - 2006, when the leadership viewed largely unrestrained financial markets as their own best supervisor.

If the creators of the Fed thought that a centralized authority would prevent the occurrence of future problems in the financial sector of the economy, they were of course wrong. October 1929 saw a financial panic of epic proportions and the commencement of a decade that would be known as the Great Depression. Particularly following Franklin Roosevelt's ascendancy to the Presidency in 1933, the prevailing government attitude became one of activism. Between 1932 and 1940, a host of oversight efforts for the financial system became law (see Appendix A). These laws were amended significantly in the following decades, and new measures enacted to meet new situations. For example, controls on interest rates, which were included in the New Deal laws, proved over the years to be cumbersome and anticompetitive. A 1980 law began their phase out.[5] As another example, restrictions on interstate bank offices were largely lifted by a 1997 law.[6]

But from the New Deal laws of the 1930s through the first decade of the 21st Century—a period of almost 80 years—the basic oversight structure for the financial industry changed only incrementally. The structure rested on four pillars: disclosure, regulation-supervision, limits on activities, and decentralization. Disclosure means revealing an institution's financial status, such as its balance sheet and income statement. Disclosure in some degree applies not just to financial institutions but to publicly traded non-financial companies as well. Broadly defined, disclosure includes the prevention of financial fraud, most of which is due to inadequate or purposely misleading disclosure.

Regulation-supervision means the establishment of rules for an industry and scrutiny of the companies in the industry to ensure that the rules are adhered to. The depository institutions industry—commercial banks and thrifts, the latter term referring mainly to savings and loan associations and credit unions—is among the most heavily regulated-supervised industries in the economy, if not the leader.

Activity limitations confine most types of financial institutions to financial activities, and in many cases to particular types of financial activities. For example, banks themselves—not necessarily their parent holding companies—have generally been confined to the taking of deposits and the making of loans.

Lastly, decentralization meant that there was no supreme authority. Regulation-supervision was in the hands of a number of independent or largely independent government agencies. The jurisdiction of each agency extended only to a segment of the financial industry, and sometimes only to particular activities. In many instances, states also had a hand in the game. (see Appendix B).

Gaps and Ideology

The oversight structure that existed from the 1930s to 2010 worked well enough for much of the period, but inertia was a problem. The oversight structure's details tended to become solidified. Significant adjustments did not usually result from foresight but from an occurring or imminently pending crisis. Decentralization meant that both the Big Picture and new types of financial activities received insufficient attention. It was too easy for government entities to say either "keep your hands off my turf" or "not my problem." Subsectors of the financial industry, and individual companies, exploited the oversight decentralization to mitigate bothersome restraints. An industry subsector and its regulator oftentimes developed too cozy a relationship, hindering effective oversight.

Technological changes could render a portion of the existing regulation-supervision system ineffective, sometimes very quickly. Products, companies, and industries very similar to those that were regulated and supervised but that legally lay just beyond the then-current regulation-supervision system could appear. Money market funds, credit default swaps, and hedge funds are examples of financial innovations that developed largely beyond the boundaries of the regulation-supervision that existed at the times of their appearance.

Similarly, activity limitations needed periodic adjustments to address changes wrought by technology. An example of an activity adjustment that was in fact made involved the Glass-Steagall Act. That Act, a part of the Banking Act of 1933,[7] successfully separated commercial banking and investment banking activities for a number of decades. Commercial banks could not offer the securities origination and placement services that constitute much of investment banking, and investment banks could not engage in a central commercial banking function—the taking of deposits.

As the end of the 20th Century neared, however, the main effect of Glass-Steagall appeared to have become negative: it was hindering efforts by segments of the financial industry to adjust to an environment being radically changed by technology. Commercial banking activities and investment banking activities were increasingly losing their distinctiveness. Acquiring funds through borrowing was no longer a simple choice between two well-defined alternatives: receiving a loan (from a commercial bank) or selling bonds (through an investment bank). The initial debt obligation had become just the start of a process that could involve loan sales to third parties, securitization in many forms and at various levels, hedging, derivatives, and so on. In this world, Glass-Steagall was ineffective at best and more often an obstacle to competition. The new world of financialization certainly needed oversight and control, but a law passed in 1933 to control Industrial Age financing was not the answer. Glass-Steagall was repealed in 1999 by the Gramm-Leach-Bliley Act.[8]

As a general result of Gramm-Leach-Bliley, banks, insurance companies, securities firms, and other financial institutions can affiliate under common ownership. The common ownership is a financial holding company. The major activities limitation that remains today is a prohibition on the mixing of banking and commerce. In other words, a bank and an institution outside the financial industry cannot normally be under common ownership.

In addition to gaps in the oversight structure that develop because of the inexorable imperative of technological change, there was—and is, and will likely remain—the role of ideological rigidity and stagnation. Take the Brooksley Born saga mentioned in Chapter 1.[9] In 1996 Born was appointed Chairman of the Commodity Futures Trading Commission by President Bill Clinton. She developed concerns about the growing derivatives market, particularly the over-the-counter, and thus largely unknown, segment of the market. Among the derivatives of interest were credit default swaps. Born wanted to take a formal look at what was going on, at what dangers might be lurking, and by early 1998 was pushing the matter hard.

But her efforts came to naught. Standing in defense of the status quo, in defense essentially of not wanting to know what was going on, of what dangers might be lurking, were fellow members of the President's Working Group on Financial Markets: Federal Reserve Chairman Alan Greenspan, Treasury Secretary Robert Rubin, and Securities and Exchange Commission Chairman Arthur Levitt, Jr. Their opposition appears to have been a combination of regulation-supervision rigidity, Good Ol' Boy obtuseness, and ideology. Derivatives fell largely beyond existing regulatory-supervisory schemes. As a female and a newbie to a government position, Born was an outsider. But ideology was probably the controlling factor. Greenspan was a fervent believer in the desirability and efficacy of market self-regulation, and the other members of the Working Group, and their staffs, were not far behind. Congress sided with the Good Ol' Boys, eventually passing a moratorium on any CFTC action regarding swaps, including even examining the market and issues. Not only did ideology triumph, but also anti-intellectualism. Born left the CFTC in 1999.

Until the collapse of 2007-08, ideology continued to prevent any serious look at a possible need for more oversight of derivatives. Senator Phil Gramm, a skeptic of much regulation-supervision, was Chairman of the Senate Banking Committee in the very early part of the decade. And the eight years of George W. Bush's Administration were not a period of regulatory-supervisory zeal. Unfettered markets were viewed as the ideal. Calls for expansion of government involvement in markets were generally not well received.

Reform, 2010 Style

The collapse of 2007-08 forced a hard look at the financial industry oversight structure that had existed in basic form since the 1930s. The result, after considerable debate on both broad political philosophy and intricate details, was the Dodd-Frank Wall Street Reform and Consumer Protection Act.[10] With President Barack Obama's signature on July 21, 2010, Dodd-Frank became the law of the land.

How to summarize an 848-page (single-spaced) law? Well, an initial point to mention is that many regulations will be necessary before much of the law becomes, well, law. One law firm estimated that Dodd-Frank calls for 243 explicit rulemakings; also, 67 one-time reports or studies.[11]

But two broad generalizations can be made about what the law attempts to do. First, Dodd-Frank attempts to centralize the decentralized oversight structure that governed the financial industry for almost eighty years. Second, Dodd-Frank attempts both to improve the regulation-supervision of elements of the financial industry already subject to oversight and to bring regulation-supervision to the many oversight gaps that developed during the latter decades of those eighty years.

In the near-term, the second generalization might be the most important. Imposing a degree of oversight on the elements of dark money and the shadow banking system—swaps, hedge funds, and the like—and more oversight and control on the standard banking system, might rein in, at least for a time, the attitudes and practices that brought on the Great Recession. In addition to swaps and hedge funds, specific topics addressed by Dodd-Frank include (the list is only partial) the TBTF (Too Big To Fail) quandary, the insurance industry, clearing and settlement systems, consumer protection, rating agencies, proprietary trading by banks (the Volcker Rule), bank capital, and systemic risk. Regarding the specific topics, Congress left many details to the oversight agencies, both individually and jointly. How successful the agencies will be in producing regulation-supervision that strikes an appropriate balance between oversight and the marketplace is a big unknown. The efforts will indeed be interesting.

But as important as actions on the many individual targets might be, the centralization of the oversight system could well prove, over the long-term, the most significant aspect of Dodd-Frank. Centralization that does not succumb to bureaucratic rigidity and inertia, or to an ideology of the market is always right, has the potential to prevent the development of oversight gaps flowing from overly exuberant financial innovation.

Dodd-Frank has sixteen titles. The core of the Act's centralization of financial industry oversight is Title I, Financial Stability.[12] A new entity, the Financial Stability Oversight Council is created. Its voting members are ten in number and are the honchos of the major financial offices or agencies: the Secretary of the Treasury, who is the chairman; the top individual of the Federal Reserve, OCC, SEC, FDIC, CFTC, FHFA, NCUA, and Bureau of Consumer Financial Protection, a new office created by Dodd-Frank; and an independent member with insurance expertise. It also has five nonvoting members: a state insurance commissioner, a state banking commissioner, a state securities commissioner, and the Directors of two new offices created by Dodd-Frank: the Office of Financial Research and the Federal Insurance Office. Now really, with such a group being required to meet, discuss, and make decisions and recommendations, and if bad things still happen, is there any hope?

Title I specifies three purposes and fourteen duties for the Oversight Council.[13] The three purposes are: (1) to identify risks to the financial stability of the United States that could arise from the material financial distress or failure, or ongoing activities, of large, interconnected bank holding companies or nonbank financial companies, or that could arise outside the financial services marketplace; (2) to promote market discipline, by eliminating expectations on the part of shareholders, creditors, and counterparties of such companies that the Government will shield them from losses in the event of failure; and (3) to respond to emerging threats to the stability of the United States financial system. Purposes 1

developments. Homeland security is the locus of one such effort. The Department of Homeland Security was authorized by the Homeland Security Act of 2002 and became operational in January 2003.[16] A raft of federal entities were wedged into a single organization. The federal entities pretty much kept their original functions and jurisdictions, however, with the result being more layers of bureaucracy for coordination and oversight purposes. Fortunately, or maybe not, there was a tool to aid the coordination and oversight: the computer.

How about national intelligence? Prodded by the terrorist attacks of September 11, 2001, Congress acted upon a long-considered idea to add a degree of centralization to the nation's intelligence efforts. The result was the Intelligence Reform and Terrorism Prevention Act of 2004.[17] The act created the Office of the Director of National Intelligence with coordination and oversight responsibilities for the various agencies, offices, and service organizations in the nation's intelligence community. As in the case of the Department of Homeland Security, the various agencies, offices, and service organizations pretty much kept their exiting missions.

Thus complexity of human efforts and organizations appears to be a component of the Information Age. The computer has brought about complexity, is a tool for attempting to control complexity, and is a creator of additional complexity. Where this complexity spiral takes economics, governing, markets, politics, and much else is, to revert to a cliché, anybody's guess.

So one factor in Dodd-Frank's success, failure, or something in between will be its complexity. If something too complex for humans to implement and manage has been created, the act will be ineffectual at best. But if the computer provides a tool for timely and sufficient command and control, then Dodd-Frank might one day be labeled a success. A crucial factor will be whether or not the new Financial Stability Oversight Council is actually able to oversee and coordinate the many established, venerable institutions—with their Type A personality leaders—theoretically under its umbrella.

In addition to just plain complexity, the implementers of Dodd-Frank face other obstacles. One is resistance by the private sector elements that are the object of oversight. Some of these elements, such as commercial banks, have long been a central focus of the financial oversight system and have often successfully resisted components of that system. For others, such as brokerage houses, oversight has existed but has not been as extensive. For still others—those in the dark money game or constituting the shadow banking system—oversight is a new, and not welcome, reality. The shadow banking system—hedge funds, various derivative creators, investment banks, and similar entities—will likely do their collective damnedest to avoid as much outside scrutiny as possible.

Two topics illustrate the challenges that face the implementers of Dodd-Frank. The proprietary trading activities of banks are curtailed in Dodd-Frank by the so-called Volcker Rule, named after former Federal Reserve Board Chairman Paul Volcker. The rule prohibits any "banking entity" from engaging in proprietary trading, or sponsoring or investing in a hedge fund or private equity fund. Precisely, or even generally, what and who the rule covers, however, will depend upon implementing regulations. Big bucks are involved, which means lobbyists, horse-trading, cajoling, and both reasoned and hyperbolic argument. The rule is not effective until 2012, and that will just be the start of a two-year transition period.

The second illustrative topic involves the concept of Too Big To Fail, or TBTF. Beginning with the rescue by federal regulators of Continental Illinois National Bank and Trust Company in 1984, at the time the seventh largest bank in the nation, the Too Big To Fail debate has bedeviled Congress, regulators-supervisors of the nation's financial system, policy makers responsible for the nation's general economic health, commentators, and academics.[18] A good part of the problem with the debate is the collision of a catchy made-for-sound-bite slogan—Too Big To Fail—with Information Age economic and political complexities. The brevity and pithiness of the slogan implies a policy or practice that can be easily changed. But the slogan belies the economic and political difficulties and tradeoffs involved in decisions about government intervention to prevent possible financial chaos when very large private sector businesses get into trouble.

Dodd-Frank wisely avoids the misleading phrase "Too Big To Fail." The act does, however, attempt to establish procedures for dealing with large institutions whose collapse would have economy-wide reverberations. Title I includes provisions about identifying and overseeing what summaries of the act refer to as "systemically important" banking and financial organizations. Title II sets forth "Orderly Liquidation Authority" for certain financial companies. But Dodd-Frank's contributions have neither halted use of the Too Big To Fail slogan as a great sounding but highly inaccurate way of referring to the issues, nor produced a consensus that anything has significantly changed.

For example, Sheila Bair, Chairman of the FDIC, one of the few government officials to foresee the problems of 2007-2009, and arguably someone who should be discouraging policy-making-by-sound-bite, has credited Dodd-Frank with "empowering the government with the means to end Too-Big-to-Fail."[19] On the other hand, Robert Shiller, Professor of Economics and Finance at Yale University, prolific writer, and someone who also warned of the coming financial debacle, has been reported as contending that Dodd-Frank did not solve the problem of Too Big To Fail. Although impressed by Dodd-Frank, Shiller was quoted as saying at a conference: "What we've seen so far is not going to eliminate the problem of systemic risk, because it's a very difficult problem. It involves the nature of the banking system, which is inherently vulnerable....It's vulnerable to runs and collapses, just like steam engines are vulnerable."[20]

Money Creation—The Ultimate Problem?

But perhaps the ultimate determinant of Dodd-Frank's success, and of humankind's efforts to prevent financial collapse in the Information Age, will be the money creation problem. The growth of financial assets—both standard credit and equity instruments and the new world of derivatives—in the thirty or so years since the inception of the Information Age is really just a growth of money expansively defined. Margin, debt, credit and equity instruments, the many forms of derivatives, they are not included in the basic money supply M1 and M2, but at a broad level they are forms of money. And their values are variable, extremely at times. And the computer has made them so darn easy to create.

Once upon a time, money was something tangible, gold and silver coins for example. The appearance of paper bank notes still maintained the tangibility connection. But then concepts of debt, credit, and fractional reserve banking brought something else, something more ephemeral. Money could be just entries in an accounting system. The Information Age brought more abstraction, much more. Money and accounting systems could take the form of bits and bytes in the ether. And money could be created or destroyed with the click of a computer key.

As money progressed from the tangible to the intangible, overseers of the financial system developed tools to maintain control. Perhaps the most notable of the tools was capital ratios. In essence, capital ratios mean ephemeral money has to be backed by a certain percentage of less ephemeral money. Dodd-Frank attempts to buttress the system of capital ratios. But the speed of the computer and the ingenuity of financial engineers mean effective oversight and control of the financial system will be a constantly evolving target. In economics and finance, the Brave New World might be a very messy, disruptive, chaotic place indeed.

Appendix A: Major New Deal Financial Laws

1932: The Federal Home Loan Bank Act established the Federal Home Loan Bank Board and the Federal Home Loan Bank System to increase liquidity and mortgage availability by providing funds to building and loan institutions.

1933: The Home Owners' Loan Corporation Act created the Home Owners' Loan Corporation to afford relief to distressed homeowners and provided for the chartering of federal savings and loan associations; the Securities Act of 1933 required disclosure of pertinent information regarding debt and equity securities sold in interstate commerce or through the mails; the Banking Act of 1933 created the Federal Deposit Insurance Corporation, created the Federal Reserve Open Market Committee, and placed national banks on a par with state banks with respect to branching within a state; the Glass-Steagall Act, which was four sections of the Banking Act of 1933, prohibited certain combinations of investment banking and commercial banking activities.

1934: The Securities Exchange Act of 1934 extended the disclosure principles of the Securities Act of 1933 to debt and equity securities already outstanding if listed on national exchanges; the Federal Credit Union Act provided for the establishment of federal credit unions; the National Housing Act created the Federal Savings and Loan Insurance Corporation.

1935: The Banking Act of 1935 made the 1933 deposit insurance plan for banks permanent, broadened the powers of the Federal Reserve System, and strengthened the power of the Federal Reserve Board in Washington at the expense of the Federal Reserve District Banks.

1940: The Investment Company Act provided for SEC regulation of investment companies; the Investment Advisers Act provided for SEC regulation of investment advisers.

* * *

Appendix B: Financial Industry Oversight Structure, Pre-2010

(With Some Mention of 2010 Changes)

Federal Reserve Board: The Fed was created in 1913. In addition to being responsible for monetary policy, the Fed oversees bank holding companies and financial holding companies, and state banks that are members of the Federal Reserve System.

Federal Deposit Insurance Corporation: Established in 1933, the FDIC provides deposit insurance for deposits in all banks and thrifts, national and state, and oversees state banks that are not members of the Federal Reserve System.

Office of the Comptroller of the Currency: Established in 1863, the OCC, an independent agency in the Treasury Department, oversees national banks.

Office of Thrift Supervision: A successor to the Federal Home Loan Bank Board (FHLBB), which was established in 1932 and legislatively terminated in 1989, the OTS oversaw federal thrifts, and savings and loan holding companies; the OTS was within the Treasury Department; the Dodd-Frank Wall Street Reform and Consumer Protection Act of 2010 provided for the termination of the OTS and the transfer of its functions to the other banking agencies (OCC, FDIC, and the Fed).

National Credit Union Administration: The successor to a bureau established in 1934, the NCUA oversees federal credit unions and provides deposit insurance to both federal and state credit unions through the National Credit Union Share Insurance Fund.

Federal Financial Institutions Examination Council: Established in 1979, the FFIEC is an interagency body empowered to establish uniform principles, standards, and report forms for the examination of financial institutions by the Fed, FDIC, OCC, OTS, and NCUA.

Federal Housing Finance Agency: Another successor through several iterations of the FHLBB that was established in 1932, the FHFA was created in 2008 through a merger of the Federal Housing Finance Board, the Office of Federal Housing Enterprise Oversight, and an office of the Department of Housing and Urban Development; the mission of the FHFA is to provide effective supervision, regulation, and housing mission oversight of Fannie Mae, Freddie Mac, and the Federal Home Loan Banks.

Department of the Treasury: Established in 1789, the Department of the Treasury is a cabinet-level agency with a broad portfolio concerning the nation's economic and financial systems.

Securities and Exchange Commission: Established in 1934, the SEC has the primary responsibility for overseeing the securities industry, including the stock exchanges, and enforcing the securities laws.

Commodity Futures Trading Commission: Established in 1974 as a successor to an oversight system for the trading of agricultural commodities, the CFTC oversees futures and options markets.

President's Working Group on Financial Markets: Established by Presidential Order in 1988 to make recommendations regarding the stock market chaos of late October 1987, the Working Group consisted of the Secretary of the Treasury and the Chairmen of the Federal Reserve Board, the SEC, and the CFTC; since then, the Working Group has provided a forum for interagency consideration of financial industry oversight matters.

States: For banks, thrifts, and credit unions, the states charter and oversee institutions that are also subject to a degree of federal oversight by one or more of the federal agencies (a situation known colloquially as the dual banking system); prior to the Dodd-Frank Wall Street Reform and Consumer Protection Act of 2010, no federal agency had the primary responsibility of overseeing insurance companies, their oversight being left to the states and to what was required by the federal securities laws.

* * *

Notes

1. Welcome to the Information Age

1. *The Financial Crisis Inquiry Report: Final Report Of The National Commission On The Causes Of The Financial And Economic Crisis In The United States,* January 2011.
2. Frank Partnoy, "Washington's Financial Disaster," *The New York Times,* January 30, 2011, Week in Review, p. 9.
3. Allusions to big picture, macro-level matters are not wholly absent from *The Financial Crisis Inquiry Report.* For example, an incident is described on page 17 concerning a paper presented at a conference in Jackson Hole, Wyoming, by Raghuram Rajan, who was then on leave from the University of Chicago's business school while serving as the chief economist of the International Monetary Fund. The paper was entitled "Has Financial Development Made the World Riskier?" Rajan told the Commission in testimony that the attendees, including then-Harvard President Lawrence Summers, reacted largely with scorn to the topic. The Commission's report seemed critical of the attendees' negative reactions. But the macro-sounding topic itself apparently did not rouse the Commission's interest.
4. See, for example, Princeton University's WordNet: http://wordnet. princeton.edu (accessed January 2, 2011), where Information Age is defined as "a period beginning in the last quarter of the 20th Century when information became easily accessible through publications and through the manipulation of information by computers and computer networks." The term, of course, is susceptible to other chronological definitions. For some purposes, the Information Age could be dated to the first electronic computers (late 1930s through the 1940s), or even to the invention of the electrical telegraph (1830s). But the term as used in this book refers to

the recent decades when the information storage and processing power of the computer have become widely available to businesses and individuals.

5. The sectors of the economy considered in this book are those in the Flow of Funds Accounts compiled by the Federal Reserve Board. The Flow of Funds Accounts are published quarterly. The Accounts are divided into three broad categories: domestic nonfinancial sectors, domestic financial sectors, and foreign (or more formally, rest of the world). The domestic nonfinancial and domestic financial sectors are further broken down. The domestic nonfinancial sectors are household, nonfinancial corporate business, nonfarm noncorporate business, farm business, state and local government, and federal government. In the domestic financial sectors are twenty sectors. The more recognizable include commercial banks, savings institutions, credit unions, various types of insurance companies, finance companies, mutual funds, money market mutual funds, government-sponsored enterprises, and issuers of asset backed securities. In this book, the singular terms "domestic financial sector" or just "financial sector" refers to the plural "domestic financial sectors" in the Federal Reserve Flow of Funds Accounts.

6. http://www.answers.com/topic/financial-engineering, accessed January 2, 2011.

7. Available in early 2011 at http://test.business.illinois.edu/finance/areas.aspx?code=E, accessed January 2, 2011.

8. Ibid.

9. David Warsh, "State of Financial Engineering," The Boston Globe, January 17, 1988, p. 73.

10. Google exercise performed January 2, 2011. The news archive search tool could be found in early 2011 at Google>News>About Google News (tab at bottom of News page)>News archive search (tab Learn more). See also John F. Duffy, "Why Business Method Patents?", November 6, 2009, available at SSRN: http://ssrn.com/abstract=1501317, accessed January 2. 2011.

11. Susan F. Rasky, "Brady Sees No Urgency To Put Curbs On Buy-outs," *The New York Times*, February 1, 1989, Section D, p. 2.
12. Warsh, note 9.
13. United States Department of the Treasury, *Report of the Presidential Task Force on Market Mechanisms* (also known as the Brady Commission Task Force Report), Washington, D.C., January 1988.
14. Warsh, note 9.
15. *Ibid.*
16. H.M. Markowitz, "Portfolio Selection," *The Journal of Finance*, 7 (1) (March 1952), pp. 77-91.
17. Fischer Black and Myron Scholes, "The Pricing of Options and Corporate Liabilities," *Journal of Political Economy*, 81 (3) (1973), pp. 637–654.
18. Robert C. Merton, "Theory of Rational Option Pricing," *Bell Journal of Economics and Management Science*, 4 (1) (1973), pp. 141–183.
19. "Baruch MFE excels," News release, September 3, 2008, accessed January 2, 2011, http://mfe.baruch.cuny.edu/features.
20. See the website of the International Association of Financial Engineers for a partial listing of universities that offer financial engineering and related programs: http://iafe.org/html/about_introduction.php, accessed January 3, 2011.
21. Warren Buffett, *Berkshire Hathaway Inc. 2002 Annual Report*, p. 15, accessed January 2, 2011, http://www.berkshirehathaway.com/2002ar/2002ar.pdf.
22. Justin Lahart and Jon Hilsenrath, "'Titan of Economics'," *The Wall Street Journal*, December 14, 2009, p. A5.
23. L. Gordon Crovitz, "In Finance, Too, Learning Entails Risk," *The Wall Street Journal*, April 20, 2009, p. A13.
24. *Ibid.*
25. "Paul Volcker: Think More Boldly," Interview, *The Wall Street Journal*, December 14, 2009, p. R7.
26. Edmund L. Andrews, "Greenspan Concedes Error on Regulation," *The New York Times*, October 24, 2008, p. B1.

2. Financialization

1. Albert M. Teplin, "The U.S. Flow of Funds Accounts and Their Uses," *Federal Reserve Bulletin*, July 2001, pp. 431, 434.
2. See Zoltan Pozsar, Tobias Adrian, Adam Ashcraft, and Hayley Boesky, *Shadow Banking, Staff Reports no. 458*, Federal Reserve Bank of New York, July 2010.

3. The Computer

1. Alan Greenspan, Remarks on "Banking Supervision" before the American Bankers Association, Washington, D.C., September 18, 2000, accessed January 5, 2011, www.federalreserve.gov/boarddocs/speeches/2000/20000918.htm.
2. Cameron L. Cowan, Statement before the Hearing on Protecting Homeowners: Preventing Abusive Lending While Preserving Access to Credit, Subcommittee on Housing and Community Opportunity, Subcommittee on Financial Institutions and Consumer Credit, U.S. House of Representatives. November 5, 2003, accessed January 5, 2011, www.house.gov/financialservices/media/pdf/110503cc.pdf.
3. *Ibid.*
4. *Ibid.*, which reports that first CMO was issued in 1983.
5. *Ibid.*, which reports that the first ABS was issued in 1985.
6. Wikipedia places the first CDO issuance in 1987, accessed January 5, 2011, http://en.wikipedia.org/wiki/Collateralized_debt_obligation.
7. Neil O'Hara and Anthony Currie, "Securitization's $8.7 Trillion Challenge," *American Securitization*, Winter/Spring 2009, pp. 32-38, at 34.
8. *Ibid.*
9. "The gods strike back" in "A special report on financial risk," *The Economist*, February 13, 2010, p. 3 (of the special report section).
10. Kara Scannell, "At SEC, Scholar Who Saw It Coming," *The Wall Street Journal*, January 25, 2010, p. C1.

11. Henry Hu, "Empty Creditors And The Crisis; How Goldman's $7 Billion Was 'Not Material'," *The Wall Street Journal*, April 10, 2009, p. A13.

12. That general principle did not prevent the rise of a life insurance secondary market in which individuals, mostly elderly, purchased polices on their own lives and then sold the policies to investors. *See* Leslie Scism, "Insurers Sued Over Death Bets," *The Wall Street Journal*, January 3, 2011, p. C1.

13. "Over the counter, out of sight," *The Economist*, November 14, 2009, p. 93.

14. Joe Nocera, "Risk Management," *The New York Times Magazine*, January 4, 2010, p. 24.

15. Board of Governors of the Federal Reserve System, "The Supervisory Capital Assessment Program: Design and Implementation," April 24, 2009, accessed January 5, 2011, http://www.federalreserve.gov/newsevents/press/bcreg/bcreg20090424a1.pdf.

16. *The Economist*, note 9, p. 6.

17. *See* Zoltan Pozsar, Tobias Adrian, Adam Ashcraft, and Hayley Boesky, *Shadow Banking, Staff Reports no. 458*, Federal Reserve Bank of New York, July 2010.

18. "New Bank Rules Sink Stocks," *The Wall Street Journal*, January 22, 2010, p. A1.

19. Susan Pulliam, Randall Smith, and Michael Siconolfi, "U.S. Investors Face An Age of Murky Pricing," *The Wall Street Journal*, October 12, 2007, p. A1, Table entitled "Source of Uncertainty."

4. Capitalism on Steroids

1. Niall Ferguson, *The Ascent of Money* (The Penguin Press, New York, 2008), p. 49.

2. For an analysis supporting these contentions, see Luiz Carlos Bresser-Pereira, "The Global Financial Crisis and a New Capitalism?", Levy Economics Institute of Bard College, *Working Paper No. 592*, May 2010.

5. Patents and Finance, Say What?

1. For sources and discussion on early English and U.S. patent law, see the concurring opinion of Judge Dyk and the dissenting opinion of Judge Newman of the U.S. Court of Appeals for the Federal Circuit in the case of *In Re Bilski*, 545 F.3d 943 (Fed. Cir. 2008).
2. Ch. 11, §1, 1 Stat. 109, 110 (1790).
3. Ch. 11, §1, 1 Stat. 318, 319 (1793).
4. *Diamond v. Diehr*, 450 U.S. 175, p. 182 (1981).
5. 35 U.S.C. §101.
6. Concurring opinion of Judge Dyk in *In Re Bilski*, 545 F.3d 943, p. 966 (Fed. Cir. 2008); for a contrary view, see the dissenting opinion of Judge Newman in the same decision (pp. 976-998).
7. *Ibid.*, Judge Dyk, p. 974.
8. *Diamond v. Chakrabarty*, 447 U.S. 303, p. 309 (1980).
9. See Justice Stevens' dissenting opinion in *Diamond v. Diehr*, 450 U.S. 175, pp. 193-220 (1981), for a review of the early history of patents and computer programs.
10. *Gottschalk v. Benson*, 409 U.S. 63 (1972); *Parker v. Flook*, 437 U.S. 584 (1978); *Diamond v. Diehr*, 450 U.S. 175 (1981).
11. The Court of Appeals for the Federal Circuit (called the Federal Circuit or CAFC) was created by Congress in 1982. The court was the result of a merger of the U.S. Court of Claims and the U.S. Court of Customs and Patent Appeals (CCPA). Among other things, the Federal Circuit's jurisdiction includes certain patent matters.
12. 149 F.3d 1368, p. 1375 (Fed. Cir. 1998).
13. Class 705 does not capture all applications concerning business methods; classification is an art, not a science.
14. USPTO, *Automated Financial Or Management Data Processing Methods (Business Methods)*, A White Paper, 2000, accessed January 6, 2011. http://www.uspto.gov/patents/resources/methods/whitepaper.pdf.
15. 545 F.3d 943 (Fed. Cir. 2008).
16. *Ibid.*, p. 954.

17. 130 S. Ct. 3218 (2010), Slip Opinion No. 08-964.
18. *Ibid.*, Opinion of Justice Kennedy, p. 12.
19. *Ibid.*, Opinion of Justice Kennedy, p. 9.
20. US 7,840,423 B2, November 23, 2010; US 7,840,467 B2, November 23, 2010; US 7,840,470 B2; November 23, 2010.
21. Found in "System and Method for Pricing Default Insurance," US 7,818,242 B1, October 19, 2010, assigned to Morgan Stanley.
22. US 7,801,789.
23. US 7,797,213.
24. US 7,263,502.
25. US 7,747,508.
26. *Ibid.*, Claim 1.
27. US 7,685,044.

6. Financialism

1. Laura LaHaya, "Mercantilism," *The Concise Encyclopedia of Economics*, accessed January 7, 2011, http://www.econlib.org/library/Enc/Mercantilism.html.
2. Paul A. Samuelson, *Economics* (McGraw-Hill, 10th ed., 1976), p. 870
3. "Data, data everywhere" in "A special report on managing information," *The Economist*, February 27, 2010, p. 4 (of the special report).
4. See, Robert J. Samuelson, "A Wall Street pay puzzle," *The Washington Post*, January 18, 2010, p. A17, for a discussion of production versus wealth.
5. David S. Holland, *When Regulation Was Too Successful—The Sixth Decade Of Deposit Insurance* (Praeger Publishers, 1998). The difficulties that banks and savings and loan associations encountered in the 1980s and early 1990s are often referred to collectively as the Savings and Loan Crisis. This is not strictly accurate because many commercial banks were also involved. Sometimes the crisis is referred to as the Thrift Crisis because of the involvement of institutions, such as mutual savings banks, that are similar to savings and loan associations. "Thrifts" is a generic term referring

to savings and loan associations, mutual savings banks, and a few similar institutions.

6. *Ibid.*, pp. 128-129.
7. Dan Baum, "The Better Angels of Our Nature," *The Washington Post*, August 23, 2009, p. B7 (In a book review of *A Paradise Built In Hell*, by Rebecca Solnit).
8. Thomas L. Friedman, "The Inflection Is Near?", *The New York Times*, March 8, 2009, p. 12 (Opinion Pages in Week In Review).
9. "Onwards and upwards," *The Economist*, December 19, 2009, p. 38.
10. Alan Borning, "Computer System Reliability and Nuclear War," in *Breakthrough: Emerging New Thinking*, Anatoly A. Gromyko and Martin E. Hellman, Editors (Walker & Company, New York, 1988), pp. 61-64.
11. *Ibid.*
12. David Hoffman, "'I Had A Funny Feeling in My Gut'," *The Washington Post*, February 10, 1999, p. A19, accessed January 7, 2011, http://www.washingtonpost.com/wp-srv/inatl/longterm/coldwar/shatter021099b.htm.
13. United States Department of the Treasury, *Report of the Presidential Task Force on Market Mechanisms* (Washington, D.C., January 1988), (also known as the Brady Commission Task Force Report).
14. "Preliminary Findings Regarding the Market Events of May 6, 2010," *Report of the Staffs of the CFTC and SEC to the Joint Advisory Committee on Emerging Regulatory Issues*, May 18, 2010.
15. *Ibid.*, p. 1.
16. "Superfast Traders' New Edge," *The Wall Street Journal*, June 4, 2010, p. C1.
17. Preliminary Findings, note 14, pp. A-2 to A-6.
18. Preliminary Findings, note 14, pp. A-10 to A-11.
19. "Suspicions Linger Over Acceleration in Camrys," *The Washington Post*, February 20, 2010, p. A-1.
20. "U.S. Absolves Toyota Electronics," *The Wall Street Journal*, February 9, 2011, p. B1.
21. National Transportation Safety Board, *Collision of Two Washington Metropolitan Area Transit Authority Metrorail Trains Near Fort Totten*

Station, Washington, D.C., June 22, 2009, Railroad Accident Report NTSB/RAR-10/02, Washington, DC.

22. Robert N. Charette, "Automated to Death," *IEEE Spectrum*, December 2009, accessed January 7, 2011, http://spectrum.ieee. org/computing/software/automated-to-death.

23. P.W. Singer, *Wired for War:The Robotics Revolution and Conflict in the 21st Century* (Penguin, 2009), and by the same author, "War of the Machines," *Scientific American*, July 2010, p. 56.

24. David Wessel, "Meet the Unemployable Man," *The Wall Street Journal*, May 6, 2010, p. A2.

25. Raymond Kurzweil, *The Age of Intelligent Machines* (first published in 1990; published by MIT Press in 1992); *The Age of Spiritual Machines* (Viking Adult, 1999); and *The Singularity Is Near:When Humans Transcend Biology* (Viking Adult, 2005).

26. http://singularityu.org/, accessed January7, 2011. *See also* Ashlee Vance, "Merely Human? So Yesterday," *The New York Times*, Sunday Business Section, June 13, 2010, p. 1.

27. From the movie *2001:A Space Odyssey*, 1968.

7. Financial Industry Oversight for the Information Age

1. Bray Hammond, *Banks and Politics in America, from the Revolution to the Civil War* (Princeton University Press, 1957), p. 103.

2. *A History Of Central Banking In The United States*, The Federal Reserve Bank of Minneapolis, accessed January 7, 2011, http://www.minneapolisfed.org/community_education/student/centralbankhistory/bank.cfm.

3. *Ibid.*

4. *The Founding Of The Fed*, The Federal Reserve Bank of New York, accessed January 7, 2011, http://www.ny.frb.org/aboutthefed/history_article.html.

5. Depository Institutions Deregulation and Monetary Control Act, Pub. L. 96-221.

6. Riegle-Neal Interstate Banking and Branching Efficiency Act, Pub. L. 103-328.

7. Pub. L. 73-66.
8. Pub. L. 106-202.
9. For a detailed review of the Brooksley Born saga, see: Anthony Faiola, Ellen Nakashima, and Jill Drew, "The Crash, Risk and Regulation; What Went Wrong," *The Washington Post*, October 15, 2008, p. A1.
10. Pub. L. 111-203.
11. DavisPolk, *Summary of the Dodd-Frank Wall Street Reform and Consumer Protection Act, Enacted into Law on July 21, 2010*, July 21, 2010, accessed January 7, 2011, https://www.davispolk.com/files/Publication/7084f9fe-6580-413b-b870-b7c025ed2ecf/Presentation/PublicationAttachment/1d4495c7-0be0-4e9a-ba77-f786fb90464a/070910_Financial_Reform_Summary.pdf.
12. Sections 101-176 of Dodd-Frank.
13. Section 112 of Dodd-Frank.
14. Section 153 of Dodd-Frank.
15. Section 152 of Dodd-Frank.
16. Pub. L. 107-296.
17. Pub. L. 108-458.
18. For a detailed discussion of Too Big to Fail, see David Holland, *When Regulation Was Too Successful—The Sixth Decade of Deposit Insurance* (Praeger Publishers, 1998), Chapter 4.
19. Sheila Blair, "Statement by FDIC Chairman Blair on Senate Passage of Regulatory Reform Bill," FDIC Press Release, July 15, 2010.
20. William Alden, "Shiller: Dodd-Frank Does Not Solve Too Big To Fail," *Huffington Post*, October 26, 2010, accessed January 7, 2011, http://www.huffingtonpost.com/2010/10/26/robert-shiller-dodd-frank-too-big-to-fail_n_774302.html.

Index

www.ingramcontent.com/pod-product-compliance
Lightning Source LLC
Chambersburg PA
CBHW070147290526
45789CB00002B/661